# Take a GOD
## Look at Yourself

# Wendy Treat

All Scripture is from *The New King James Bible* unless otherwise noted.

Verses marked NIV are taken from the HOLY BIBLE, NEW INTERNATIONAL VERSION®, NIV®, Copyright © 1973, 1978, 1984 by International Society. Used by permission of Zondervan. All rights reserved.

**Take A God Look At Yourself**
ISBN #1449986447

**Copyright © 2010 by Wendy Treat – Casey Treat Ministries. All rights reserved.**

Previously Printed As
**Mirror, Mirror On the Wall**
*Seeing Yourself Through God's Eyes*
Library of Congress Control Number: 2002094750
First Printing, September 2002
Second Printing, January 2006

Casey Treat Ministries
P.O. Box 98800
Seattle, Washington 98198
www.caseytreat.com
www.wendytreat.com

Inside chapter photos taken by Wendy Treat and friends.

# Dedication

To all of you who like me, in your journey to be all God wants you to be have had to struggle, cry, fight and almost give up hope... yet you just will not quit!

We may not have won the prizes in school, but we are winning the victory in life step by step.

I am with you!

# Contents

# Acknowledgments

When I accepted Jesus as my Savior at 17 years of age, He started me on the journey of seeing myself as He sees me. In doing this, He used many people along the way.

**To name a few of those special people:**
My parents, Pastors Paul and Virginia Peterson.
Pastors Mark and Kathy Shaw, my first youth pastors.
Pastor Roy Johnson, founder of the Bible school where I met Casey.
Julius Young, founder of the drug program from which Casey graduated, and our first true spiritual father.
Pastor Art Sather, our first pastor.
Pastors Fred and Betty Price, our pastors and constant spiritual teachers.
Dr. and Mrs. David Yonggi Cho, our role models and mentors.

Jill Cooper, Gina Pettit, Terry Schurman, Molly Venzke, Denise Llewellyn, Tammy Kallander, Tina Scott and Koren Leggett.

Top of the list, my gifts from God: Caleb, Tasha, Micah and Casey, my man!

# Introduction

Take a GOD look at yourself ...

Who do *you* see when you look in the mirror? Do you see someone with whom you would like to spend time? Someone who people like to be around and is a positive influence? Or do you feel rejected, unnecessary and in the way most of the time?

What you perceive about yourself when you look in the mirror is your self-image. Your self-image is how you see and how you feel about yourself. It's the source of how you act—toward yourself and toward others.

If you have a good self-image, you are probably kind, patient, polite, happy, outgoing, and have other similar positive qualities.

On the other hand, if you have areas of your self-image where you are not confident, you will demonstrate that. You may be frustrated, depressed, intimidated, and wonder why people do not respond to you in a positive way.

In short, your self-image—how you see yourself—controls you and your behavior.

For example, if you think you are stupid, that overwhelming image of yourself will affect your ability to reach out to people. If a person asks you a question, all of a sudden your "stupid image" pops up and your mind goes blank. Not because you don't know the answer. Many times you will know the answer, but because of your self-image, your mind will go blank instead of responding.

Or, if you see yourself as unwanted—and maybe your parents truly did not want you—that self-image will affect your own family. For instance, when your children get to the age when they want to spend more time with their friends or don't want you to kiss them good-bye in front of their friends...how do you feel? Does that threaten your relationship, or is it not a problem because you know they love you?

Maybe you feel that people do not like you. When you find out that a group of friends got together and didn't invite you, you believe it is because *no one* likes you. The truth is they probably called you, but you were not home.

In situations like these, your reactions are coming out of your poor self-image. At these moments you are feeling lack and in need of approval. You need reassurance and want to hear over and over: *"You are wanted. You are wanted."* However, the image you have of yourself is: "They don't want me."

When you are plagued by a sense of rejection or low self-worth, it is manifested in every area of your life. You will project the message, "Nobody wants me," to everyone—your parents, your husband, your kids, your friends, and even strangers. You will perceive rejection from everyone from sales people to the Fed Ex delivery man, because you look at everything in life through the eyes of your poor self-image.

Having a poor self-image controls your emotions and your behavior. In short, it controls your life.

I want to help you end the control a poor self-image has had on your life. Through taking a look at yourself through God's eyes, those negative aspects of your behavior, interactions, relationships, and spiritual walk can change. Your life will become completely different—for the better.

I want to take you on the journey I have traveled from believing I was an average, mediocre, bossy, tough, overweight person—all the labels I grew up believing, hearing, and perceiving—to realizing who I really am in Christ. Is it easy? Is it a one-time, get-fixed-quick mentality? No. But step by step, through His love and mercy, God took the negative things I believed about myself and showed me His point of view. I took a look at myself through God's eyes. It has turned my thinking around—and my life.

I experienced change.

And so can you.

Through the pages of this book, I will show you how to exchange your image for His, one step at a time.

*—Wendy Treat*

*Caleb 10, and Micah 6*

*Trained for battle - devil watch out!*

# Chapter ONE

## The Challenge of Having A Right Self-Image
*The fight has been ongoing since you were born.*

Skinny.

Fat.

Motor mouth.

Shy.

Lanky.

Stocky.

Stubborn.

Lazy.

And on and on it goes. Whatever you heard growing up is what you believed. It's who you are today. That's what a self-image is all about—believing you are a certain way, whether it is the true or not.

Webster defines self-image as "an individual's concept of himself and his own identity, abilities, worth, etc."

So, what you think and how you feel about yourself are major attributes of your self-image. The words that come out of your mouth and the things you allow yourself to do reflect how you truly see yourself.

***For out of the abundance of the heart the mouth speaks. A good man out of the good treasure of his heart brings forth good things...*** *(Matthew 12:34-35)*

Your self-image has developed from the time you were a small child. When you heard words such as timid, stupid, bossy, etc., you eventually lived up to those words. Through the words you heard you acquired a perception about yourself, and you've acted and reacted every day out of that perception in your relationships, in your jobs, in your parenting, and in your marriage—until now.

Today, as you read and apply the truths presented in this book, you have the opportunity to begin unraveling the wrong self-image that has formed over the years and start the process of change in your life.

*A smile of encouragement at the right moment may act like sunlight on a closed up flower. It may be the turning point for a struggling life.*
*- Author Unknown*

Today, if you choose to follow the instructions and wisdom found in this book, you can forever change your destiny and how you interact with those around you. You literally can make the world around you a better place for yourself.

No, you can't change everyone else. Your family and friends will remain the same. But when your self-image is what God intended it to be, nothing will look the same, and you won't behave the same, because your perception won't be the same.

I know. I've been through this process of change.

I went from being believing I was an average, bossy, tough, overweight person—all the labels I grew up hearing, perceiving and believing—to realizing who I really am in Christ. Through His love and mercy, God took the negative things I believed about myself and showed me His point of view. I began to see myself through God's eyes. It turned my thinking completely around—and my life.

Consequently, God has been able to take me into places of my destiny that I could have never reached before. He has enabled me to be a wife, even a pastor's wife, a mother, a Bible study teacher, a Christian author, and so much more. Because I allowed Him into my heart to change me, I have become more and achieved more than I ever dreamed possible.

I have overcome the pressure to perform for acceptance, the anxiety of feeling I did not measure up, and the paralyzing fear of failure.

### Not Everyone Is Going To Approve Of You

I remember when my husband, Casey, and I started our church in Seattle, Washington, more than 30 years ago. I was 22 and wide-eyed with excitement. I just knew that everyone would believe in what we were doing and be just as positive as I was. After all, our entire purpose was to help people have a better life by helping them know Jesus as their Lord and Savior. We wanted to edify people.

Was I ever wrong.

A local media reporter interviewed Casey and me about our new church. I answered all of the questions with great enthusiasm. I talked and talked and was extremely honest about how we were helping people.

I had no idea the reporter was looking for something to use against me.

When the story aired, the edited version left out what I said at the beginning and end of the interview. The only portion used was the middle of the interview, which left me sounding mean and self-centered.

I was shocked and hurt. I quickly realized that not everyone will agree with me, not everyone will like me, and not everyone will believe in me.

The change I've experienced in my life has taught me that all of that is OK.

> *A man is not hurt so much by what happens, but by his own opinion of what happens*
> *- Michel de Montaingne*

There was a time when having others' approval was extremely important to me. That was when I had a poor self-image.

Then I realized that Jesus overcame criticism, so I could too.

When Jesus walked the earth, the Pharisees didn't like Him. So ultimately, they persecuted Jesus, and they hung Him on the cross.

If people persecuted Jesus, it can happen to you—and me.

Too many people are consumed with everyone else's opinion of them—mom's, dad's, sister's, brother's, husband's, best friend's, boss's, and the list goes on. They are consumed with what others think and say, rather than with what God has said. This insecurity has mounted in their lives, and now the devil uses it against them. They are intimidated to do anything new. They can't take the risk of possible failure. They are therefore afraid to walk in the place of authority God has given them as believers.

It's obvious that not everyone will like what you and I do. So we need to have a way to succeed, despite the blows that come in life.

## The Consequences of a Poor Self-Image

The image you have on the inside of you affects your entire life. For example, if you don't know who you are in Christ, you will be easily swayed into making wrong choices. You will marry for all the wrong reasons. You will make career choices for the wrong reasons. You will miss windows of opportunity with your children. You will miss God's best. There are commands in the Scripture you won't fulfill, because you are afraid to step out in faith.

Having a poor self-image dramatically affects every

area of your life—and everyone with whom you interact.

If your self-image is low, you will not act on the Word with strength—because you will be afraid of everyone else's opinions. You will be afraid that people will say something about you, that you won't look right, or that someone will laugh at you or call you a religious fanatic. You will constantly look for other people's approval and praise.

If you have lived this way, you have allowed everyone else to develop your self-image for you. Ultimately, you have been controlled by everyone—except God.

But just as I learned from that interview, not everyone will like everything you do or say.

## My Beginning of Change

The change, from having a poor self-image to having God's image on the inside of me, began right after I was saved in my late teens. I was attending Bible College and had just started dating Casey. Growing up I always knew I was going to marry a pastor and be involved in ministry. I knew my destiny in life was to serve God and that included going to Bible school to learn more about the Bible.

One day, as I was sitting on my bed, my roommate and I were reading our Bibles together. As I was reading, the Holy Spirit illuminated a scripture in Galatians to me. It was like a light bulb went off in my head and I could clearly understand what this scripture was teaching me.

**But let each one examine his own work, and then he will have rejoicing in himself alone, and not in another.** *(Galatians 6:4)*

There has never been a scripture in my Christian walk that has affected me more than this scripture. That day, it was as if God took an arrow, pierced my heart, and said, "This is for you. I want you to understand it personally, and I want you to share it with others."

I realized that the meaning of this verse had everything to do with my self-worth—and yours—because it has to do with knowing who you are in Christ, knowing the person God created you to be, and having the confidence to be able to "rejoice in yourself."

This scripture made me begin to look at who I was. I began to examine myself to see who I *really* was, not just the image I projected publicly. I began to look at my heart.

As I did, I discovered I really wasn't tough...as I had believed and acted. I realized that I didn't want to be that way, and I wanted to stop portraying that image to everyone I met.

The more honest and vulnerable I was with myself, the more I began to see things in a different light—in the light of God's Word and His love. I discovered that inside I was truly a kind person who wanted to help others.

I found myself excited about the good that God saw in

me! I saw something positive in myself. I saw that there was more value deep within me than that "toughie" I showed on the exterior.

Because of how this scripture has worked in my life through the years, I have succeeded in fulfilling my destiny. I'm doing what God has called me to do up to this point in my life—and it is so satisfying and peaceful!

## We All Have Issues

When *you* know who *you* are in Christ, you can walk in your destiny. When you see who you really are—who God created you to be before you were ever conceived—it will be like standing before a dessert buffet hearing God say, "Go ahead, have it all. You can have all of My characteristics on the inside of you!"

Now, I was raised in a pastor's home. My parents loved God, served God, and did all they could to help people. They loved me as well, and gave me the best of what they had to give emotionally, physically and spiritually.

*Treat people as if they were what they ought to be and you help them become what they are capable of being.*
*- Author Unknown*

But in spite of all my advantages, I still had issues to deal with in seeing myself as God does. I still had issues to deal with in learning who I was in Christ and embracing that in my heart.

This is because your self-image really

14

isn't based on what your parents did or didn't do right. It isn't based on the abuse, rape or incest you experienced. It isn't based on the adultery you committed or the marriage you lost.

It's based on how the devil used every situation—every opportunity—in your life to steal from you who you really were created to be.

Satan is your enemy, not mankind.

Satan has worked to steal from you through peer pressure, parental influences, siblings, teachers—virtually everyone who ever repeatedly said anything negative to you.

In most cases, these people weren't mean or bad. In their hearts, they were not being evil. They were just being brothers or sisters, mothers or fathers, and teachers or friends who were dealing with their own insecurities. Unfortunately, they said negative things to you so often that it built a belief system in you about who you are.

Whatever you heard about yourself....too fat, too skinny, too tall, too short, bossy, timid, stupid...if you have never discovered who you are in Christ, you are *living those* words today. You are living with a poor self-image—created by the devil, himself.

It's time for you to deal with those issues and take back your life. It's time you experience a change in your thought patterns and beliefs. Line up everything with God's Word and His love.

I want to help you fulfill your destiny on this earth—
and it will take a healthy, godly self-image for you to do
that. You are a gift. And you *have been given* gifts and
talents. You have a purpose to fulfill—even if you were
labeled an "accident." Even if you were told cruel things
that made you feel unwanted, God has always wanted
you! Jeremiah 1:5 promises, ***Before I formed you in the
womb I knew you; before you were born I sanctified
you; I ordained you a prophet to the nations.***

Because you heard negative things said so often, you
accepted them as your own, but they are not yours to
have. Those negative words belong to the devil. Refuse to
accept them as your own! See who you are in Christ, and
walk in all that God has planned for you.

To get there, you have to be willing to change—and I
will teach you how. I will walk with you down the road I
have traveled...from the prison of a poor self-image to the
exhilarating freedom of knowing who you are in Christ.

It is then that you can be all you were created to be.
Then, and only then, can you take a look at yourself
through God's eyes.

## Confess God's Word Over Yourself Today!

Confessing God's Word - His promises - over yourself will strengthen you. As you see yourself differently, you will act differently. Here is a confession you can begin to use in your own life. You can add more scriptures or change some to fit your needs. At the end of each chapter I have included personal confessions from my family and friends. I encourage you to find a confession that works for you, or to use these to create your own.

*I am a disciplined woman of God. I love the Lord my God with all my heart, all my soul, and all my mind. I am not conformed to this world, but I am being transformed by the renewing of my mind. I set my mind on those things that are true, honest, just, pure, lovely, of good report, virtuous, and praiseworthy. I prosper and live in health even as my soul prospers. I am strong and very courageous. I am like a tree planted by the rivers of water; whatever I do prospers and is blessed. I am a woman who loves the Word. I seek first God's kingdom and everything I have need of is added into my life. I love being a wife, a mom, a pastor, and a friend. I give of myself to love and minister to those in my life. I study the Word and I am fulfilling the call of God in my life.*

*—Wendy Treat*

❖ I am a new creature predestined for greatness. (II Corinthians 5:17)

❖ I am forgiven and will not be tormented by my past errors. (I John 1:9)

❖ I am a giver and God is causing people to help me prosper. (II Corinthians 9:5)

❖ God is on my side. I choose not to fear. (Psalms 118:6)

❖ The Holy Spirit is my Helper. I am never alone and I have the peace of God. (Philippians 4:7)

❖ I am blessed and it's a matter of time before things change. What I see now is only temporary. (Ephesians 1:3; II Corinthians 4:18)

❖ I hear the Father's voice; the voice of a stranger I will not follow. (John 10:5)

❖ My steps are ordered by God. (Psalm 37:23)

❖ Abundance is God's will for me and I will not settle for less. (John 10:10)

❖ I am an overcomer and my faith is changing my circumstance. (1 John 5:4)

❖ I am loved by God regardless of how I perform. (Romans 5:8)

❖ I am a child of God, fully accepted by the Father. (John 1:12)

❖ I have authority over the devil and no demon power can hurt me. (Luke 10:17)

# Questions To Consider

1. What are some of the negative thoughts you have had about yourself?

2. Who are some of the "very important" people you influence during your day?

3. Find and write out a scripture based on who you are in Christ.

Tasha, age 6

*I might be missing a couple teeth right now but my mom thinks I'm cool!*

# Chapter TWO

## You Are Not Perfect...
### *But You Are Perfectly Designed By Christ*

I grew up with two sisters who were long, lanky and thin. You know...the kind of girls who never need to be photo-shopped. Sadly, that's not me. Not only did I not have a long, lanky body, there was nothing I could do to make that happen. Lanky was never going to be a word to describe my body type.

Through the years of living with sisters who had "perfect" bodies, I thought over and over, *I wish I could look like them.* Every time I saw them my thoughts were consumed with, *why don't I look like that?*

Truth be told, this is something we all have done in one way or another. We have looked at someone else and thought they are smarter, prettier, thinner, and so on. We compare ourselves to others, and though we know it's wrong, we do it anyway. Comparing ourselves with others is a bad habit we have been practicing for thousands years.

Gideon, an Old Testament military hero who delivered

Israel from oppression, was also guilty of comparison. Even as God instructed Gideon in how to save Israel, he was wrestling with seeing himself as God saw him.

> ***Then the LORD turned to him and said, "Go in this might of yours, and you shall save Israel from the hand of the Midianites. Have I not sent you?" So he said to Him, "O my Lord, how can I save Israel? Indeed my clan is the weakest in Manasseh, and I am the least in my father's house."*** *(Judges 6:14-15)*

Gideon saw himself as *the least of the least!* He saw himself as the least of all the clans and the least in his family. He looked at the outward circumstances, the way he had been raised—all the comparisons in the natural realm—and defeated himself before he ever got started! He looked around at the situation, at himself, and then said, "No, way, God! I can't do it!"

Despite one success after another in defeating the Midianites, Gideon's battle with his self-image raged. Each time, even though God told Gideon He would be with him, Gideon asked God to prove Himself. He didn't believe God's Word.

How many times have you faced one glorious opportunity after another only to run from them? You lacked self-confidence because you had a poor self-im-

*A life of faith… enables us to see God in everything and it holds the mind in a state of readiness for whatever may be His will.*
*- Francois Fenelon*

22

age, which in turn fueled your habit of comparison.

Like Gideon, you have the idea that the Word is true for everyone else, but not for you. You believe the "least of the least" picture you have on the inside of you instead of God's Word. Because of comparison, you sabotage your own success. You stay weak when you compare yourself to someone else rather than rejoicing in who God has made *you* to be.

You may not see yourself correctly, but God sees you as you really are—just like He saw Gideon filled with power, not as the least of the least.

God sees you as a good speaker, a kind and gentle woman, a fabulous hostess, a loving mother, a devoted wife, a motivated household manager, an asset to your company, and more! He sees you as He made you to be—a success!

## Comparison Pushes You Away

As adults, one of my sisters and I had an interesting conversation. I shared with her my secret wish to be a long, lanky girl—and she shared hers...she had always wanted arms and legs just like mine!

We went back and forth comparing our attributes and what we wished we had. It was quite comical—and futile—for we could do nothing to change the structure of our bodies or our unique personality traits!

God does not want us to compare ourselves with anyone, because He made us exactly as He wants us to be. Not perfect, but perfectly designed by Him. Comparison only distracts us from what we are to be doing in our lives. It takes away from thinking positively and living a life that blesses others. In fact, the Bible tells us if we compare ourselves to others we are unwise.

*For we dare not class ourselves or compare ourselves with those who commend themselves. But they, measuring themselves by themselves, and comparing themselves among themselves, are not wise. (II Corinthians 10:12)*

Comparing yourself to anyone else will never get you anywhere...and it's destructive. It damages your self-image and consequently, your relationships with other people.

For example, instead of loving and appreciating my sisters, my thoughts were focused on wanting to look like them. I convinced myself their looks were better than mine. And since I thought they looked better than me, how could I ever like them? How could I ever rejoice with them? How could I ever have a good relationship with them?

In short, comparison is ugly. It pushes people away from you—and it pushes you away from your destiny.

## Least of the least or warrior in the Spirit?

It just amazes me how God made us each as individuals. No two of us are alike! If God somehow created every person on earth completely unique from anyone else how can we say that one is better than another? And if one is not better than another, why would we compare ourselves with anyone else?

As a believer, every one of us has a different role, a special gifting, a unique calling on our lives (I Corinthians 12:11-22). You aren't supposed to be like anyone else or do what God has called *them* to do. We each must accept the role that is ours.

> *All that I have seen readies me to trust the Creator for all I have not seen*
> *- Ralph Waldo Emerson*

When we first began our ministry, like Gideon, I began to think of myself as not quite right for the role God had placed me in. In my mind I wasn't quite good enough. When situations arose at church, I would often respond too quickly, rather boldly and not always kindly.

Then I would feel bad and tell Casey he had married the wrong woman. I would say, *I'm not a pastor's wife. I'm not loving and kind enough.*

Sounds like, *I'm the least of the least!* doesn't it? Can't you just see me with my head hanging down and my sad face?

Casey would always laugh. He saw me as God saw me. He saw God's picture of who God said I was, even though I didn't.

Today, I can look back and laugh, too. Casey would go bananas with anyone but me. He needs a wife who is quick and bold, who acts the way I do. Of course, as I've matured I have learned how to be a little slower to answer in some situations. On the other hand, I also see that the bent of my personality is the very thing needed to complete my husband. I am needed in our church, and I am the one God placed here to help bring about what He has called us to do.

To get where I am today in my destiny, I had to see and accept who I was in Christ, and quit seeing myself as not good enough.

I have learned to fight to overcome a wrong self-image. But I didn't do it by comparing myself to others. I did it by warring in the spirit.

When you have a warring spirit, you fight the battle in the realm where it really exists. You don't fight against flesh and blood—against your family members or your brothers and sisters in Christ. You fight according to Ephesians 6:12: *For we do not wrestle against flesh and blood, but against principalities, against powers, against the rulers of the darkness of this age, against spiritual hosts of wickedness in the heavenly places.*

Comparison will defeat you. But warring in the spirit against the devil and his schemes will bring victory. As you begin to pray and confess God's Word over your life instead of focusing on the negative thoughts of comparison, you will win the battle.

## The Plague of Insecurity

If comparison is eating you alive, insecurity is really the plague stealing your life.

Most people look for security by trying to figure out what other people have, how they look, who they hang with. Then they want what those other people have. That's not rejoicing over what they have been given. That way of thinking produces a pattern of lack and insecurity.

*God has said we are accepted according to what we have. For if there is first a willing mind, it is accepted to what one has, and not according to what he does not have. (II Corinthians 8:12)*

So, what do *you* have? That's what God will judge you by. He will never judge you for not doing something that was someone else's responsibility. I know for certain that I will never stand before God and hear Him say that I failed because I didn't teach piano lessons! What a joke! I am not supposed to teach piano lessons. I am not proficient in any area even related to music.

Your destiny is linked with what you already have. It's linked to the gifts and talents God has given *you*—not to what anyone else has been given.

I remember as I was growing up people would comment on how I always like to tell others what to do. I've always had that bent to my personality. Even today, I like taking charge, telling people what to do, and teaching the first five people I run into the latest thing I've learned. If I see a new movie, read a great book or hear an encouraging story, I can't wait to tell others about it.

That's my personality—but I didn't always see it as positive. I perceived it as bossy. I saw it as a negative personality trait. And you can be sure a few people along the way reinforced my negative thinking.

So, I tried to be like other people, even like Casey.

The first time I heard Casey preach, we were at Bible College in a class where you learned how to put sermons together. When he spoke, I was so impressed. He was only 20, but I thought he was the best teacher I'd ever heard in my entire life. (I was only 18 then, but I still think he's the best!)

Later, when I began teaching, I tried to be just like Casey. I thought his way was best—well thought-out and practical. His notes were color-coded. They were organized perfectly. So, I watched Casey, compared myself, and decided his way was better than mine.

Why? I didn't know how to rejoice in myself. I only saw my weaknesses. I only saw the things I did not have. I felt insecure. I did not *know* the Word which says, **My grace is sufficient for you, for My strength is made perfect in weakness.** *(II Corinthians 12:9)*

So, you guessed it! I tried having him put my notes together for me!

Obviously, it didn't work. I was so frustrated! I got lost in the notes and became so confused. I couldn't do it that way, because I was trying to make Casey's gifting mine. And because of that I failed. Not in the calling on my life to teach the Word, but in trying to do it the way Casey did.

I quickly gave up trying to be like Casey (to the relief of those listening!) and discovered my own style of teaching. It was inside of me all along. I began to learn what God said about me and discovered that my personality was perfect for what God had called *me* to do - to teach, to mother, to co-pastor and so on. I discovered that my personality—which I had perceived as negative—was a gift from God for leading people.

I discovered who I was in Christ.

By choosing to be all that God has called you to be and accepting your personality traits you will burst out of your insecurity, obey God's Word and fulfill your destiny.

In fact, God has commanded you to love yourself. Matthew 22:37-39 commands us:

*'You shall love the Lord your God with all your heart, with all your soul, and with all your mind.' This is the first and great commandment. And the second is like it: 'You shall love your neighbor as yourself.'*

The Word teaches you to love your neighbor as yourself. If you cannot love yourself, you cannot love anyone else. A right self-image has nothing to do with pride. But it has everything to do with love.

## Rejoice in the Differences

When you realize the power, blessings and fulfillment that come from being who you are, you can enjoy who everyone else is—just like God does. He loves you as much as the person you think is prettier, more together, more successful, and smarter than you. Learn to enjoy the differences between people. Enjoy the differences between you and your siblings, your husband, your co-workers, and your friends.

For example, we have three children, and they are all different, but all equally valuable in our eyes. We enjoy all of them.

Caleb, our oldest, is so unique. He is very aware of people and situations. He sees the big picture many times, and he can seem very quiet. He is very perceptive and sees things about people and situations that are very deep.

Tasha is more like me—talking, moving, and having trouble sitting still in school. I always earned a zero in self-control! She did not get a zero because she was more disciplined than I was, but she is very outgoing. She tells you exactly what you should do, how you should do it, and wants you to take care of it *right now*. She's very much her own self and very unique.

Micah is our youngest. Every person he meets, he physically touches in some way. He reaches out to people everywhere he goes. Micah will meet a stranger and the stranger will feel like he's known Micah all his life. That's

Micah's personality bent.

Just as I look at my three children and see all of their differences, so God looks at us and sees our differences, too. And just like I love the gifts and talents God has put in each of my children, God loves what He has put into you.

I don't have a favorite among my kids. God doesn't have favorites either. God looks at you and me and your children and friends, and He sees the differences in each one of us, yet loves us all the same. Each one has been gifted and called. Each of us is unique and special in His sight.

I Corinthians 12:4 tells us, ***There are diversities of gifts, but the same Spirit.***

We are supposed to be different. My children have the same parents and live in the same environment with similar friends, but they are very different. You are supposed to be different, too.

### The Anointing Is On Who You Are

Someone once said to me, *Remember the anointing is on who you are, not on who you're trying to be.* Those gifts and talents within you are who you are. When you operate in them, God can anoint you and what you're saying. When you operate in them, God can truly use you. He needs your anointed personality traits on this earth to fulfill His will.

When God looks at you He sees the *real you*, and He

31

accepts you based on that. So accept who you are.

Challenge the voice in your head that puts you down and compares you to everyone around you.

Challenge the words that have held you captive for so many years.

## Overcome the Naysayers

We've all been impacted by negative words. A teacher once told me I would never be a good writer. I took that to heart and it dominated me for years. I believed and acted out of that belief as I told myself, I can't write. I can't write.

How like the enemy to use words so connected with my destiny in God. If I had not laid hold of the truth and begun to understand that what God says is higher than what any person says, I would have never written any of the books I have. It's a part of my destiny. I am called to help and serve people—and writing books is part of that!

Using God's Word, I uprooted those negative words that were planted in me, so I could walk in my destiny.

Whatever negative words have been spoken over you, God wants to uproot them by His Spirit and His love. He does that by teaching you understand and apply His Word. As He told Gideon, He is also telling you the truth about yourself so that you can fulfill His will for your life. With His Word you can fulfill your destiny and walk those paths that have appeared too hard for you in your own strength and ability.

## U—B—U!

The greatest calling on your life is to be the best you there is. Galatians 6:4—the foundation for this book—set me free to be the best me I can be: ***But let each one examine his own work, and then he will have rejoicing in himself alone, and not in another.***

In examining myself, I had to stop looking at other people, comparing myself to them and with what I considered to be ideal. Something inside of me made me think that I wasn't smart enough. In reality, I don't have the ability (or the desire) to be a brain surgeon or a judge. I am not an analytical type of thinker. But because of my perception, I judged that type of occupation as smart, and, since I don't have the ability for those occupations, I judged myself as not smart. And, since I couldn't do either of those jobs, I decided I also couldn't do any of the other things I had thought about.

How the enemy deceives us!

God never said I had to be smart in just one way. All He wants is for me to be smart in my gifts and callings. He wants me to do my best to walk in the ability that He put within me. I don't have to be smart in any of those other realms. I am just one piece of the whole puzzle that He has anointed on the earth today.

As a member of the human race, just do your part by

using the gifts and talents God has put within you. You don't have to be anything or anyone else!

In learning to accept yourself, learn how to rejoice in the person you are, and stop looking at what you don't have. You have to stop being jealous of what other people have. Stop thinking in terms of smarter or better or more.

If you were supposed to be what other people are, the ability to do it would be within you.

Now, I'm not talking to you if you have the ability, but just haven't attained the training you might need. I'm talking to you if the root to your issues is your self-image...and its ability to sabotage your success.

God's design is for you to combine the gifts and talents He has given you with the training you need to perfect them so that you can glorify Him and serve the world. Remember, God has accepted you.

***For if there is first a willing mind, it is accepted according to what one has, and not according to what he does not have.*** *(II Corinthians 8:12)*

Accept yourself.

Renew your mind according to God's Word.

Learn who you are in Christ.

And experience an entirely new life seeing yourself through God's eyes—full of worth and value as who you really are.

## Confess God's Word Over Yourself Today!

*I am a mighty woman of valor. I am strong and very courageous. I can do all things through Christ who gives me strength. Though I walk into the valley of the shadow of death I will fear no evil for You walk with me always. I am a giver for I know I will reap what I sow. I give with great love, for I know I am giving to the Father of all fathers. I am a Proverbs 31 woman. A virtuous woman is a precious jewel so I strive daily to be a virtuous woman. For You know the thoughts You have toward me. Thoughts of peace and not evil. Thoughts to give me a future with great hope. And I strive always to have Your thoughts and not my own. I know why I am here. I am here for two reasons: to love God and to fulfill Matthew 28:18 to go and make disciples of all the nations, baptizing them in the name of the Father, the Son and the Holy Spirit. I am not flavorless for I am bold with a great passion for the lost.*

*–Tasha Treat*

# Questions to Consider

1. What is your "picture" of yourself? Write a brief description.

2. How have you limited yourself—seen yourself as "the least of the least"?

3. What are some ways you have compared yourself with others?

4. Who have you been warring against in the flesh lately? (people, situations)

Tasha, age 1

*Makeup, curlers, shopping...*

Tasha, age 5

*...isn't it great being a girl!!!*

# Chapter
## THREE

### The Original Image
*What you were created to have and how to get it.*

I was a middle child of six kids—pastor's home, normal family, with no abuse or problems that would get me on any talk show today. When I was born again at 17, God began to deal with me. I recognized that I didn't have any huge problems, but in my mind there wasn't anything special or great about me either. Consequently, I didn't feel especially good about myself.

Alas, I had grown up as Miss Average. I had never achieved anything. I had never excelled or been pushed to be all I could be in any realm. There was never any sense of destiny or drive. I just lived a ho-hum, boring kind of life.

Many people settle for this same kind of life—even if on the surface they have pursued and achieved a successful career.

Picture it: they go to work, come home, eat dinner, watch TV, have a couple of kids, go to the ball game, and one day, life is over.

This is not God's best.

Life is about so much more. It's not about existing. It's about soaring. God is way too creative, too big and too loving to just want you to hang around on earth waiting to die so you can go to heaven.

He has a much greater purpose for you. So, don't be satisfied with where you are. Don't let your present self-image keep you at the present level.

Go for more!

There is a destiny to fulfill—your destiny. What you see in yourself may only be seed form and those seeds may not have begun to blossom yet. Or, they may have begun to develop small shoots, but aren't fully developed at this point.

Whatever stage of growth you are at, it's time to cultivate your seeds to full maturity. If you'll be faithful to let God continue to work in you, then a gorgeous fully grown flower will emerge...and you will walk in your destiny.

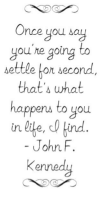

*Once you say you're going to settle for second, that's what happens to you in life, I find.*
*- John F. Kennedy*

### The Right Self-Image

When you walk in your destiny, every season of your life has meaning—every part of your life has purpose.

Part of my destiny in years past was to know who I was in Christ so I could be a better mother to my three children. If I had not known who I was in Christ,

I would not have known how to raise them God's way. I would have been debilitated from fulfilling my destiny in that area of my life.

But through the understanding of the Word, God has enabled me to fulfill that area and many other facets of my destiny. God has restored to me the right self-image He created me to have.

Genesis 1:26-27 reveals the origin of the image God created just for you. It is extraordinary to say the least:

*Then God said, "Let Us make man in Our image, according to Our likeness; let them have dominion over the fish of the sea, over the birds of the air, and over the cattle, over all the earth and over every creeping thing that creeps on the earth. So God created man in His own image; in the image of God He created him; male and female He created them.*

Your self-image has been created in the image of God Himself. He is your Heavenly Father, and He sees you as His child.

God created you to have dominion on this earth, and to never be dominated by the circumstances surrounding you.

Taking it a step further—you are never to be dominated by the lies of the devil. You are never to be dominated by thoughts that you are not appreciated, by all the negative words spoken over you, or by your wrong self-image that has developed over the years.

You are to be dominated by the Word of God, and who He says you are...

**You are more than a conqueror.** *Yet in all these things we are more than conquerors through Him who loved us (Romans 8:37).*

**You are wise, righteous and sanctified.** *But of Him you are in Christ Jesus, who became for us wisdom from God—and righteousness and sanctification and redemption (I Corinthians 1:30).*

**You are a new creation.** *Therefore, if anyone is in Christ, he is a new creation; old things have passed away; behold, all things have become new (II Corinthians 5:17).*

**You live by faith.** *I have been crucified with Christ; it is no longer I who live, but Christ lives in me; and the life which I now live in the flesh I live by faith in the Son of God, who loved me and gave Himself for me (Galatians 2:20).*

**You were chosen before the foundation of the world.** *Just as He chose us in Him before the foundation of the world, that we should be holy and without blame before Him in love, having predestined us to adoption as sons by Jesus Christ to Himself, according to the good pleasure of His will (Ephesians 1:4-5).*

**You were saved by grace through faith.** *For by grace you have been saved through faith, and that not of* *yourselves; it is the gift of God (Ephesians 2:8).*

And that is just the tip of the iceberg. *There are hundreds of scriptures with the phrase "in Christ" or "in Him" that reveal who you are in Christ if you are born again.*

Being born again, accepting Jesus as the Lord and Savior of your life, being filled with the Holy Spirit, (because you need His help) and then learning who you are in Christ is the very foundation of a godly self-image. It is the only foundation that will hold up through the trials of life.

The world's foundation won't hold you up. The world tries to find self-worth, but it is a labor done in vain. The world's results are short-lived and limited to man's natural ability.

God's image, on the other hand, is limitless and filled with His goodness.

When you are born again, you become re-created—a new creation in Christ Jesus as mentioned in II Corinthians 5:17—in the image of God. He comes to live within you in the person of the Holy Spirit. John 14:16-17 is a promise Jesus has kept to this day:

***And I will pray the Father, and He will give you another Helper, that He may abide with you forever—the Spirit of truth, whom the world cannot receive, because it neither sees Him nor knows Him; but you know Him, for He dwells with you***

***and will be in you.***

You do not know the fullness of God's image until you begin to read and digest God's Word and what it says about you. The Holy Spirit, your helper who lives in you will illuminate the Word and teach you from it.

Until you renew your mind to think what the Word says about you, your old self-image, created by whatever the devil has thrown your way will dominate you.

Romans 12:2 instructs you:

***And be not conformed to this world: but be transformed by the renewing of your mind, that you may prove what is that good and acceptable and perfect will of God.***

> My mother taught me very early to believe I could achieve any accomplishment I wanted to. The first was to walk without braces.
> - Wilma Rudolph

The devil has worked hard to make sure you are conformed to this world. He has been out to destroy you, your family and your health since the beginning of time. He wants to steal your self-image every single day. If you try to step out and do something new or good, the devil will bombard you with thoughts of fear, failure, and insecurity. The devil comes immediately to steal what you have accomplished, what you are attempting to do, or even what you think you can do.

Jesus taught this and it is recorded in John 10:10:

44

*The thief [the devil] does not come except to steal, and to kill, and to destroy. I [Jesus] have come that they may have life, and that they may have it more abundantly.*

Satan is cunning. He comes to strip you of your identity. He comes to steal the person you are and the unique, beautiful qualities God has put within you. He comes to steal your potential.

I know that sometimes, when I want to do something new, the devil tries to mess with my thinking to remind me of those who have said, "You can't do that."

I'm sure he does this to you, too. "You'll never make it. Just give up. It's foolish to think you can achieve that."

He is so subtle. By coming in through your thought life, you naturally think those thoughts are your own, and you accept them as your own. You believe them to be truth.

But you can rise up to combat his destructive efforts.

If you will rise up and discover from God's Word who you are in Christ, you will begin to transform your self-image into His image. You will recognize the authority, love and goodness—and the gifts and potential—God has put within you.

Then, you can speak to *those* thoughts, refuting the devil's thoughts with the Word of Truth of who you really are. As you begin to act on that identity, the devil will begin losing battle after battle after battle—and you will win the war.

## All Things Are Possible

Now, as you think about this, "impossible" may be what comes to mind. Fight that hopeless thought with the Word: ***Jesus said to him, 'If you can believe, all things are possible to him who believes' (Mark 9:23).***

That is the truth. All things are possible to those who believe. *All things.*

His image is your image.

What is true about Him is true about you—and that is what you should think.

For example, if I say, "God is rich and He wants to meet all your needs," and you think, *that's impossible for me. You don't know my financial situation. You don't know what I've come from and what I've gone through.* You need to fight those thoughts with the Word, and renew your mind. That's an area where you need to change... because you are made in His image. He is rich, and He really does want to meet your needs.

> ***For you know the grace of our Lord Jesus Christ, that though He was rich, yet for your sakes He became poor, that you through His poverty might become rich.*** *(II Corinthians 8:9)*

> ***And you shall remember the LORD your God, for it is He who gives you power to get wealth, that He may establish His covenant which He swore to your fathers, as it is this day.*** *(Deuteronomy 8:18)*

46

He owns the cattle on a thousand hills (Psalm 50:10); the streets of heaven are pure gold and He even has gates each made out of a giant pearl! (Revelation 21:21)

The truth is we can't even imagine the beauty and splendor of the things God has created. He is rich and prosperous. When you look at the world around us, the water, the flowers and trees, God's beauty is everywhere.

He is the God of abundance, which covers every realm of our lives. Even the earth is His and all its fullness (Psalm 24:1). You can't get any richer than that!

And He wants you to be rich, because you are His child and made in His image. He wants you to see yourself as He is.

God has given you life, compassion, grace, and salvation. He is your example of what you are supposed to be, regardless of how you feel.

For example, you may not feel like a giver. Sometimes you may just want to keep everything for yourself. Personally, I've had to work hard naturally and spiritually to be a more giving person—financially, socially, and physically.

I came from a very non-touching, non-hugging family. You could feel the uptightness in the air. I was taught to be a non-physical giver. Now, no one taught this with words, but the actions in our home conveyed it. Therefore, I didn't grow up with the right image in this area of my life.

47

But the Books of Luke and John both say that God is a giving God.

*Give, and it will be given to you: good measure, pressed down, shaken together, and running over will be put into your bosom. For with the same measure that you use, it will be measured back to you. (Luke 6:38)*

*For God so loved the world that He gave His only begotten Son, that whoever believes in Him should not perish but have everlasting life.*
*(John 3:16)*

God gives all the time. So I've had to renew my mind to a right self-image—one that's a giver.

You may have been raised in a family where you never heard words of encouragement. You never heard words that built you up and told you how wonderful you were. If so, that is something you will have to learn to do for others.

The bottom line is, whatever you lacked growing up is now a weakness in your life—and you have to change that area of your self-image. We all have changing to do.

In her book, *You Are Somebody*, Cheryl Prewitt-Salem tells the story of how when she was getting ready for the Miss America pageant, her front teeth were temporarily bonded together because of an accident. They couldn't put braces on her teeth because it would break the bond and adversely affect her mouth. She couldn't believe she was going to the Miss America pageant with crooked teeth. And when she looked in the mirror, she saw that she still had hundreds of scars on her face. But she determined in her heart that what she didn't see, others wouldn't see either. She didn't see herself with a scarred face or with crooked teeth.

And since she didn't see herself that way, she didn't project herself that way.

As she mentally and spiritually prepared herself to step out in front of the cameras, she remembered a childhood friend who didn't have any fingers and who had club feet. Cheryl didn't realize that her friend was handicapped until her friend's mother pointed it out to her six months into their friendship. Cheryl had simply never noticed. Her friend played the piano and did everything as if she had fingers. She had worked on her image so she didn't project herself as handicapped.

> *A winner is someone who recognizes his God-given talents, works his tail off to develop them into skills, and uses these skills to accomplish his goals.*
> *- Larry Bird*

Cheryl remembered her friends' example, used it, and became Miss America while having crooked teeth and hundreds of scars on her face. She projected confidence and a positive self-image and that is what others saw!

How people perceive you is developed through what

you speak with your words or convey with your actions. How many times have you spoken the same negative things over yourself that others have said, and then told everybody else all of your negative qualities? Some of us even appear to have a sense of pride for them, when instead we should not even acknowledge them.

God does not say to applaud our weaknesses. He says we are to copy Him!

Our goal is to conform to the image of Jesus Christ. We should want to have our concept of ourselves, our identity, and our abilities wrapped up in the image of Jesus Christ. Then we'll see, feel and act as Jesus did on this earth.

## Focus on the Positive!

I want to grow and change my image to be like the image of God and of Jesus Christ. But if all I do is concentrate on my negative traits, it won't work. That's what we give off to people when we say; *I don't do that very well. Don't you know I can't do that? Did you see how overweight I am? Didn't you see how straight my hair is?*

One time, I told one of the women in our church how great she looked, but she was embarrassed because she didn't have her mascara on yet. I had to look really hard because I hadn't noticed.

How often do you tell others what's wrong with you?

Another time, at a woman's seminar, the teacher was

talking about how to be beautiful, and she said, "Not one of you noticed that my earrings do not match!" (Try this sometime. I did and no one noticed! I had been so concerned thinking that everyone saw all my flaws, only to be proven wrong.)

The speaker went on to say that we are so bound up in ourselves that we think everybody notices everything about us. So because we are so focused on the negative, we tell everybody that we think might notice. Then that's all they think about, too.

Why do we rush to present the negative side of our image to the whole-wide world?

Once, a woman who was a speaker on a panel discussion at one of our women's meetings had a cold sore on her lip. She was very sensitive about it, to the point of not wanting to be a part of the panel. She asked me to tell everyone before the discussion started that she had a cold sore. I did, but when I moved to where the audience was sitting, I couldn't see it. She knew she had an "ugly" spot, so she brought attention to something no one else could even see.

We are to conform to the image of Christ, but so often we tell everyone all about our negative qualities or the qualities that are not what they should be.

I hear women do this all the time regarding their spirituality as well. "Oh, I don't pray enough."

I am amazed at the intimidation level of women spiritually. Some women say to me, "I don't study enough."

I say, "How many times do you sit in the church service?"

"Four services a week."

Are you kidding me? With that kind of knowledge of the Word, they could go anywhere in the United States or anywhere in the world and teach the Bible. They could lead Bible studies and share so much wisdom with others. Yet they put themselves down.

Most Christians have a poor self-image of being ignorant. We tell ourselves; *I don't know enough about the Bible. I didn't go to school. I don't have all the background I need. I'm not a Bible teacher.*

I once read an article about a well-known woman who said she was not a good Bible teacher because she didn't go to Bible school. She teaches all the time and has made a tremendous difference in the lives of people around the world. As I read her comment I thought, *"Who made the rules?"* Is that the image that God gave her? What about the gifts and calling of God on her life?

Always challenge yourself: is that God's image of me? Is it my own? Or is it the devil's negative thought, *You can't do that because. . .* In reality, who is giving you your image?

You have been created in the image of God. Everything

you think should go through the filter of that image. You have to judge: Is that God's way? Is it the devil's way? Is it my old thinking? Or is that the way I was taught to think?

Ask yourself: *What kind of man was Jesus on this earth?* You are to follow in His footsteps. He is your Source of life, your Source of direction. You are to conform to His image.

Remember Genesis 1 says that you have been created in the image of God, and that is the image you are to follow in every area of your life.

When you want to know how to think in a certain area of your life, examine the life of Jesus. For example, what was Jesus' social image? What did He show us by His example on earth? How was He involved with people?

In the gospels, Jesus tells stories or parables and then He explains them. He taught repeatedly and trained the disciples and the multitudes. People came to Him, and He had compassion to teach them.

So, in your social life, God's image needs to be your image. How does God act socially? A clear picture can be seen through Jesus and the many illustrations of how He lived while on earth. You are to act the same way.

What kind of social life did Jesus have? He was surrounded by friends. At the Last Supper there was a strong relationship between Jesus and His disciples. Oh, how they loved Him and He loved them. He had people saying they would go wherever He went. He chose people and He put Himself out to be with those people. He was around many types of people. He was involved in many social occasions and fed the thousands who followed Him.

How often do you invite guests to your home for dinner? Some people don't invite friends over because they say, "we don't have time." Is it really time that holds you back?

Too often the image that we have of ourselves socially is that we are the bottom of the barrel. We don't have Jesus' image in us concerning our social life, our relationships with people, or our friendships. In many areas of our lives our image is, "I can't." Jesus' image was to find a need, pray and take care of it.

In my own life, there are times that I just feel grumpy, and then I get a phone call from a friend who says she really needs some help and I want to say, *"So do I."*

That's what I want to say, but my image needs to be conformed to the image of Jesus Christ, so what was His example for me to follow? In my hurt, give. In my depression, give. In my low times, give. That's the example I choose to follow.

When the disciples needed anything, they rested on Jesus. And when parents brought their children to Jesus, the disciples said, "No," but Jesus said, "Bring the little children to Me."

Jesus social life was filled with compassion—and people, people, people. He drew people to Himself. Is that your image of who you are on this earth? Or are you always afraid of people?

## A Right Self-Image Isn't "Higher Consciousness"

In dealing with your self-image, one of the things I want to very clearly state is that I do not believe in the philosophy that says, "Get yourself together, and you'll be God." Some religious or "spiritual" groups say you'll get better and better and higher in your consciousness until you eventually become God.

If you're getting confused about whether or not something is false religion or a positive self-image, understand that the devil knows that there is excellent teaching in the Bible. He knows the Word and he trembles at it. He knows that there are things in the Word that will work, so why not distort it and use it for his glory and for his power to bring people into his kingdom?

He wisely takes some of the truth from the Bible and through deceived and lost men and women he twists it just enough to cause people with a little bit of God-consciousness in them to blindly accept a lie. (II Peter 3:16)

Then they soon believe that they can be like God. But it is pride in people that causes them to want to be above everyone else—and like God. That's why so many people are deceived with a lie.

As Christians, we have to recognize that we are not God,

but rather we are made in the image of God. God wants us to see ourselves in a true light and not think more highly of ourselves than we ought to think (Romans 12:3), nor does He want us to think of ourselves as something lowly, that He didn't create us to be.

There are many vain philosophies—not just religions—

*In reality, who is giving you your image? Is it God? - Author Unknown*

that will deceive you and take you the wrong direction. For example, there are a lot of positive thinking tapes, and they say if you will listen to them, you'll be stronger in your own authority and self. You'll be a winner, and so on.

I'm sure some of those tapes have helped a few people. They've listened to the tapes and possibly stopped doing a few negative things, and started to do some positive things. But that foundational philosophy doesn't lead to life. If you're not saved, yet you are listening to a lot of positive thinking tapes, and you start acting nicer than you did last week, you are still spiritually dead.

Unless you are born again and have the life of God on the inside, you are working on a self-image that can never be what God wants. You cannot conform yourself to His image in the power of your flesh. Only when you are born again and submitted to His Holy Spirit, can He begin a work of change in you that is eternal.

Believing on the Lord Jesus Christ is the only way to

salvation for every part of you—spirit, soul and body—which includes your self-image.

> *That if you confess with your mouth the Lord Jesus, and believe in your heart that God has raised Him from the dead, you will be saved. For with the heart one believes to righteousness and with the mouth confession is made to salvation.* *(Romans 10:9-10)*

Forget humanistic philosophies and man-made religions.

Yield to the Spirit of the Living God so you can experience real life—filled with the fullness of God Himself.

> The Lord works from the inside out. The world works from the outside in. The world would shape human behavior, but Christ can change human nature.
> - Ezra Taft Benson

### Positive Thinking Will Never Be Enough

There are strengths God has put within you, and those are good. Then there are non-strengths and "learned weaknesses," such as laziness, a lack of discipline or fear that you need to challenge.

Challenge those learned weaknesses that have been incorporated into your personality from peer pressure, people's negative words, and events and places where you've been. (Casey has a powerful book, *Renewing the Mind* that deals with all of this. It will help you understand how to challenge your thinking and reprogram your mind according to God's Word. Ordering information is at the end of this book.)

The bottom line is—a right self-image is of God. But positive thinking alone will never get you where you want to be, seeing yourself through God's eyes. Positive thinking doesn't have that kind of power, because it's your own power. And your own power isn't powerful enough.

God's power, on the other hand, as your creator, is more than enough. Everything you need to succeed and to develop a right image is in Him. All love, goodness and power to walk in your destiny is in Him—and Him alone.

II Corinthians 3:5-6 says it all:

***Not that we are sufficient of ourselves to think of anything as being from ourselves, but our sufficiency is from God, who also made us sufficient as ministers of the new covenant, not of the letter but of the Spirit; for the letter kills, but the Spirit gives life.***

God is the One Who makes you sufficient—no one and nothing else.

## Confess God's Word Over Yourself Today!

*This is the day the Lord has made, I will rejoice and be glad in it! Father, I thank You that You love me with an everlasting love. Jesus Christ is my Lord and my Savior, and by His stripes I am healed and whole - spirit, soul, and body! You have given Your angels charge over me to keep me safe and protected. Father, I hunger for your Word, and I desire to study the Word to grow in my relationship with You. I am a great wife, mom and friend. I love my family and put them first place in my life after You, Lord. I have the mind of Christ and Your wisdom is formed within me. I am an able minister of the Gospel and I am called and able to do all that is placed before me. I thank You, Lord, that You bring all things to my remembrance, give me clarity of thought and wisdom in every situation I face. I am a problem solver. This is the day You have made, and I will rejoice in the great plan You have for me today!*

*—Terry Schurman*

# Questions To Consider

1. Have you confessed Jesus Christ as your Lord and Savior? If you are not sure, then turn to page 179 to learn more about this very important step in your life. It is the critical foundation to having a right self-image.

2. What are some of the negative words that have been spoken over you in the past that are affecting your future?

3. What words were spoken over you in the past that have built you up and given strength to your self-image?

4. Find a scripture, write it out and confess what God's Word says about you in one of the areas of weakness in your self-image.

Caleb 6, Tasha 4, Micah 2

*Look out giants...here we come!*

# Chapter
## FOUR

### Slaying the Giants of Your Past
*And their cohorts of rejection and inferiority.*

While renewing your mind is critical to developing a right self-image, sometimes it first takes a little excavation work before you can build a new foundation. Sometimes you have to deal with some "issues" as well.

But the good part about starting to renew your mind according to the Word is that the Word will expose where you need freedom...in your thinking, in your behavior, in your habits, and in your perceptions.

As I'm sure you understand by now, how you perceive yourself is how you will affect others and how you will give of yourself to them.

For example, if you think you are stupid, that image of yourself will affect your ability to reach out to people. If a person asks you a question, your "stupid image" pops up and your mind goes blank. Many times you will know the answer, but because of the image you have of yourself you will freeze up.

Or, maybe you're angry all the time—and you don't even know why. Looking at your past may solve the mystery. Was your father always angry, for example? Was your mother always irritated at you? Was someone always ready to pounce on you, full of explosive emotion? When someone said, "You *look* just like your dad," did you interpret that statement as "You *act* just like your dad"? Did you unknowingly take on his angry, explosive attitude? Is that why you are constantly angry and frustrated today?

Maybe your mother was a "pleaser." She cried at everything, talked to everyone, and was very emotional. And because you grew up around that, you now find yourself in the same boat.

Or, are you a person who sees yourself as unwanted—and maybe your parents truly didn't want you? That self-image will affect your own family. For instance, if your husband comes home from work tired and you have especially freshened up for him, but he just pushes right past you, sits down, grabs the newspaper, and turns on the TV, all without even noticing you. Does a feeling of anger begin to rise up on the inside of you?

Maybe you think no one likes you. So, when you find out that your friends had a party without inviting you, you believe it's because no one likes you. In reality, they probably did call to invite you, but you weren't home.

In situations like these, your reactions are coming out

64

of your poor self-image. At those moments, you are in a condition of lack and need approval. You need to be told over and over: *"You are wanted. You are wanted."* But the image you have of yourself is: *"They don't want me."*

When you are plagued by this sense of rejection, it manifests in every area of your life. You will project the message, "I'm not wanted," to everyone—your parents, your husband, your kids, your friends, and even to strangers. You will perceive rejection from sales people to the FedEx man, because you look at everything in life through the eyes of your poor self-image.

You need to look at the life lessons you grew up learning, because they still affect you today. You need to look, but not to point a finger and not to place blame. Regardless of your youth, you are responsible for your own life today. But you need to know the roots to the strongholds in your life. You need to know the roots to the poor self-image you may have—because when you have a poor self-image, it controls your emotions and your behavior. In short, it controls your life. But, understanding the reasons for your poor self-image will put you in a position to control your life as you begin to control your responses to different situations.

> One of the reasons mature people stop learning is that they become less and less willing to risk failure.
>
> – John Gardner

65

To begin experiencing change in your life, you need to start to take a look at yourself through God's eyes. As you do, you will begin to deal with the unwanted feelings within you. You'll begin to change so that you're able to respond as a child of God, rather than as someone not wanted.

### Forgiveness is critical!
A critical key to becoming free from your past is forgiving your family and yourself.

John 20:23 is vital to a right self-image: *If you forgive the sins of any, they are forgiven them; if you retain the sins of any, they are retained.*

When you forgive, you can grow. You can begin to change—step by step. The completion of change won't happen as quickly as you might want, but it will happen over time with faith and patience.

The change you experience will not always be pleasant. Growth requires pruning. Old habits, customs and routines will be cut off, and that cutting can be painful.

But you can't grow unless you allow some of the stuff that's not very pretty to come out. You have to recognize it so you can go beyond it. And you can go beyond it, but you have to be willing to fight for it and hurt a little along the way.

I've been working for several years to change some of the ways I've been programmed to behave or think that have held me down. Some of these ways I received from my parents, my sisters and brothers, my teachers, the TV or other media, but my habits can't be blamed on just one person or thing. It is a combination of people and experiences that contribute to our overall self-image.

If you're going to blame it all on just one person, then who on earth would you choose? It's impossible to figure all of that out...so don't bother. In fact, finding fault is a waste of time and energy. Just move on to the part where you get free from it all.

Think about it. My mother tried to influence me with the very best of her life and spirit. I got every good thing, but I also got every negative thing.

Do I blame my mom or do I blame my grandparents?

My grandparents, who loved God, did everything they could to influence my mother for the best. Or, do we blame the teacher who taught my mother in the 12th grade and negatively influenced an area in her life that was then passed on to me?

The maze of blaming can get very crazy. So be careful of placing the blame on everyone else. A lot of people may share the blame, but the bottom line is, *the devil is the one who came to steal, kill and destroy in your life.* So instead of looking to blame someone, start forgiving everyone—including yourself.

*You are about to experience a turning point. Stay in the game, it's too soon to quit!*
*- Van Crouch*

67

## Defeat the Giant of Intimidation

I have changed so much over the last three decades. I am so different today than I was when Casey and I began pastoring Christian Faith Center. Back then, I always felt I was the youngest of the pack. I felt so inadequate. I was 22, and even though I saw the destiny God had for Casey and me, it was intimidating. I thought, *What am I going to do? I'm not smart enough and I don't know enough yet.*

I was so intimidated that sometimes, I would become flustered when I spoke and my sentences would come out all jumbled around. I didn't know how to talk in front of people and I felt my inability so strongly.

But I chose to face the giants of intimidation and fear in my life. I chose to believe what the Word said about me, rather than my own poor self-image. I worked to overcome my feelings of inferiority.

In the Bible, King David did this very same thing. He faced a giant of intimidation named Goliath.

*The reason some people don't recognize opportunity is because it often comes disguised as hard work.*
*- Author Unknown*

In the story of David and Goliath, God gives us great understanding of how to overcome those seemingly insurmountable obstacles we face. I love reading David's response to the naysayers who told him, "You're too young, you can't do it."

*And Saul said to David, "You are not able to go against this Philistine to fight with him; for you are a youth, and he a man of war from his youth." But David said to Saul, "Your servant used to keep his father's sheep, and when a lion or a bear came and took a lamb out of the flock, I went out after it and struck it, and delivered the lamb from its mouth; and when it arose against me, I caught it by its beard, and struck and killed it. Your servant has killed both lion and bear; and this uncircumcised Philistine will be like one of them, seeing he has defied the armies of the living God." Moreover David said, "The Lord, who delivered me from the paw of the lion and from the paw of the bear, He will deliver me from the hand of this Philistine." And Saul said to David, "Go, and the Lord be with you!" So Saul clothed David with his armor, and he put a bronze helmet on his head; he also clothed him with a coat of mail. David fastened his sword to his armor and tried to walk, for he had not tested them. And David said to Saul, "I cannot walk with these, for I have not tested them." So David took them off.*
(I Samuel 17:33-39)

When you are consumed with thoughts of, *I can't. I'm but a youth. I'm not adequate for the job. I am overwhelmed and intimidated,* you have to see yourself as

David did. Even when David's brothers looked at him and said, "What are you doing here? Who do you think you are to be doing this?" he didn't receive their perception as his own.

Instead, David looked to God for his self-image, and it fueled his success. He faced and defeated the giant in his life, Goliath, and went on to be king of a nation.

Whatever your giant is, you can defeat it. Whatever is before you, if you believe God has given you a job to do, then there is always something you can do to accomplish it. You don't have to step off the path and quit the journey. Don't let inferiority derail you. Just find and do the next step toward your success.

For example, a pastor friend of mine took correspondence courses before she and her husband started their church, and she really worked hard to develop herself in the knowledge of the Word. She couldn't go to Bible school because she was raising three little girls. But she didn't let her circumstances dictate her future. She didn't allow inferiority to cripple her life.

In the same way, I keep myself growing in my destiny all the time. Every single day I listen to tapes and read something that helps me in the call God has on my life. Whether it's as a wife, a mother, or a minister, I'm learning and growing. I graduated from school, but I have not graduated from life!

To come against the inferior feeling of "I can't do it,"

you've got to rise up and see yourself as God sees you.

I heard an interview once of a young Seattle Seahawk's quarterback who did this very thing. When he was asked how was he going to play against the other great seasoned NFL quarterbacks, since he was so young, he said he had decided to take on what his opponents were saying about him to his advantage. His opponents were saying that he was really quick, good and smart. So he had decided to think about himself not as the young one, but as the really quick, good and smart one.

What a great lesson. Instead of living out of your poor self-image, take what positive things other people are saying about you and live out of that. Oftentimes, other people see attributes about you that your inferior thoughts keep you from seeing.

## Slay Your Giants

Left alone to grip you tighter year after year, inferiority will work against you day and night. It will cut off God's thoughts and God's words that come up in your mind and in your heart. It will literally steal God's life from you— His plans for you, His desires for you.

So you have to rise up big within yourself. Yes, you may be young in your spiritual walk. You may still see yourself as a little kid who can't do anything. Or, you may be a mature believer who made some huge mistakes. But only you can "slay your giant" and overcome it with the Word of God. You have to push yourself to move and go beyond what you think you can do. No one else can do it for you.

For example, I am responsible for what God has called me to do, and I can't rely on what Casey or anyone else has done. My destiny is linked with Casey's, but he could keep growing in God and I could end up paralyzed in what God has called me to do—if I let inferiority rule my life.

> The only thing that stands between a man and what he wants from life is often merely the will to try it and the faith to believe it possible.
> - Richard M. Devos

It's just like the lion and the bear that came into David's life. Rather than let them defeat him, he killed them. He didn't let inferiority keep him from killing both of them. His right self-image propelled him to overcome and fulfill his destiny.

In your Christian walk, you will be challenged. The enemy will try to stop your progress. It's inevitable. During your lifetime you will face a lion. You will face a bear. And, like David, you will only conquer them through your belief in God.

Your lion or bear could be your past—rape, incest, physical abuse, mental abuse, or a dysfunctional family situation—and all the pain that goes with it. Your lion or bear can be drugs, alcohol, pornography, sex or homosexuality.

But like David, you have to choose if you are going to

overcome or if you are going to surrender. If you are willing and obedient, you will overcome. Isaiah 1:19 says, *If you are willing and obedient, you shall eat the good of the land.*

It's clear that you have choices to make. You can stagger and allow the bear and the lion to kill you or you can see them much smaller because of your belief in God, in what He says. David saw Goliath as much smaller because of his belief in God was so big.

See your lions and bears smaller. Rather than feed garbage into your mind, plug into the holiness of God. Get His Word on the inside of you. Get His image inside of you. If you still cry over past incidents and you still feel pain from them, deal with them. Kill that lion and bear. Kill the past and quit bringing it up for the next ten years. Believe who God's Word says you are over everything else.

If you keep putting garbage in you, garbage is what will come out of you. So, change what you put on the inside of you. It is the only way you will be ready and equipped to slay the Goliaths that come your way in life.

### Whose armor are you wearing?

There are two more powerful life lessons to be gleaned from David's life. First, before David went out to kill Goliath, Saul offered his armor. David tried it on, but it didn't fit. He couldn't fight wearing someone else's gear. The

73

lesson is, he couldn't be someone he wasn't.

> *So Saul clothed David with his armor, and he put a bronze helmet on his head; he also clothed him with a coat of mail. And David fastened his sword to his armor, and he tried to walk, for he had not tested them. And David said to Saul, "I cannot walk with these, for I have not tested them." So David took them off. Then he took his staff in his hand; and he chose for himself five smooth stones from the brook, and put them in a shepherd's bag, in a pouch which he had, and his sling was in his hand. And he drew near to the Philistine".* (I Samuel 17:38-40)

You will have Goliaths to conquer in life—and you will only be able to conquer them if you know who you are. David knew who he was...and it wasn't who Saul was. Saul's armor was for Saul, not David.

No one else's armor is designed to fit you. Just like I couldn't be Casey when I preached—I couldn't put on his armor—so you can't fulfill your destiny by acting like someone else.

In the process of learning how to put on my own armor and take off Casey's, I read a book called *The Birth Order Book* by Kevin Leman. Leman's teaching helped me to quit acting like Casey in some areas where I didn't even realize how much I tried to mimic him. The book also let me see how much I had put on that wasn't *my* armor. It took me some time to get out of that armor and out of thoughts from other people's expectations—but little by little I succeeded.

And so can you. Take the time to recognize who you are. Don't be mad at your husband because you took on his armor, or mad at your friend, or that woman you have tried to emulate. Be big enough in yourself to take off their armor, whether it's the way they talk, do their hair, or wear their makeup and clothes. Quit trying to be someone else.

*Saul's soldiers thought Goliath was too big to kill. David thought he was too big to miss!*
*- Anonymous*

In the same way that Saul's armor didn't fit David physically, it also didn't fit emotionally or spiritually.

In the emotional realm, you may try to take the armor of someone of a completely different age—your friends, other teachers, other ministers, your husband, your mother, your sisters—whether they are younger or older. Don't be foolish. You are the age that you are. So, take their armor off and say, "This is what age I am and this is what I'm able to do. This is how I should act and dress." And be content and confident in that.

Or, you may be trying to put your emotional armor on someone else.

Many times, as mothers, women try to take their armor

and put it on their husbands and say, "This is how you're supposed to be." When they go out of town, they leave their husbands an entire list of how to take care of the kids. Don't do that. Let him figure it out. Let him wear his own armor and be the daddy God created him to be—not an ill-fitted duplicate of you.

I had a friend who would tell her husband, *You should do this and this and this.*

He would always respond, *You be the mom and let me be the dad.*

I've thought of that many times when I've tried to put my armor on Casey. He's not supposed to wear my armor. My children are not supposed to wear my armor. All of them have to develop their own strengths and personality styles.

## Never Lay Down Your Armor

The other life lesson we can glean from David is once you have your own armor on, don't take it off. You are who you are because God wants it that way. He wants you wearing your armor and no one else's. And, he never wants you to take it off for any reason.

David made the mistake of his life doing that very thing. He took off his armor—neglecting who he was and what he was called to do—and wound up in the wrong place at the wrong time. The result brought death, spiritually and physically, to many people.

*It happened in the spring of the year, at the time when kings go out to battle, that David sent Joab and his servants with him, and all Israel; and they destroyed the people of Ammon and besieged Rabbah. But David remained at Jerusalem. Then it happened one evening that David arose from his bed and walked on the roof of the king's house. And from the roof he saw a woman bathing, and the woman was very beautiful to behold. So David sent and inquired about the woman. And someone said, "Is this not Bathsheba, the daughter of Eliam, the wife of Uriah the Hittite?" Then David sent messengers, and took her; and she came to him, and he lay with her, for she was cleansed from her impurity; and she returned to her house. (II Samuel 11:1-5)*

When David laid his armor down at Bathsheba's feet and walked in sin, he walked away from serving God. He walked away from what he was supposed to be doing as a leader—be at war. The Bible says it was the season for the kings to go to war, but David didn't go to war. He stayed home and sent others into battle for him. He missed what God wanted him to do and got into a lot of trouble instead.

David was bored. He had done it all before, and probably felt that no one appreciated him. He was bored with the things of life. But that didn't justify not fulfilling his calling to go to war.

In a similar way, it's time for you— men and women of God—to go to war! It's time for you to keep your armor on and alleviate attitudes that will get you off the track of your destiny and into trouble:

❖ I don't like what my boss wants me to do.

❖ I don't want to work in the church nursery with the children.

❖ I'm tired of cooking and cleaning for people who don't even appreciate it.

❖ I don't want to help in the community.

❖ I've done this for ten years and no one appreciates me.

❖ I don't think anyone cares if I come or go.

Dissatisfaction can creep in at any time in life. It happened to David, the man who was after God's own heart. He grew bored and restless, laid his armor down and it led to destruction.

You can lay your armor down by being bitter, unforgiving and ungrateful for what God has done. If you are a stay-at-home wife and mother, you can become mad at your husband because he is getting all of the outside adoration and acknowledgment. Or, you may feel that he really knows the will of God for his life and you are just tagging along.

If you work outside of your home, you can become bitter

because someone else got a promotion and you didn't—when the truth is: God has something better for you.

Guard against these kinds of temptations. Stay in touch with your calling. Stay in touch with your destiny. Never lay your armor down.

And if you see someone else fall into sin, be careful to never think it couldn't happen to you.

Galatians 6:1 tells us, ***Brethren, if a man is overtaken in any trespass, you who are spiritual restore such a one in a spirit of gentleness, considering yourself lest you also be tempted.***

You may think you are strong, but you have to guard against boredom, against animosities, against feeling, "No one appreciates me." You have to guard against feeling unimportant, especially when no one is patting you on the back.

David knew who he was at one time. He slew the lion, the bear and Goliath. He was great and songs were sung about him. He walked a few more years and then, suddenly he fell into the pit.

You too can slay your lions, your bears and your Goliath, and still fall. You can walk with God, walk in the love of God, and still fall.

II Peter 3:17 warns us, ***You therefore, beloved, since you know this beforehand, beware lest you also fall from your own steadfastness, being led away with the error of the wicked.***

It is very common to get into the mundane routines of life and forget to read the Bible, pray or lift your hands to worship and love God. When this happens, your life turns into a hypocritical walk of nothingness. You walk out of the love of God and into duty and religion.

That's how every great denomination started—with people filled with great fire for God. But through too many years of doing nothing, and allowing busyness and apathetic attitudes, grumbling and complaining to come before seeking God, they fell into darkness.

So, what are you going to do? Are you going to stand steadfast in God? Are you going to follow the scripture and beware lest you fall into your own thinking?

Remember, it's not hard to fall.

One woman told me that she had a secret imagination of the *perfect guy*. She was married to a wonderful man, but she had a fantasy of the perfect guy. She was out of town, the elevator door opened, and he was standing right there. She fell just like that. Picked him up in the elevator, took him to her hotel room, and had sex. She then reaped the consequences of the pain and heartache of hurting her husband and herself. She couldn't believe she had fallen, but those few moments of sin brought about much pain. You might think that women don't fall with sexual sin. Why not? You can get wrapped up in the romance, in the sweetness of someone giving you the kind of attention your husband may not be giving you.

Beware of all the different ways you can fall. You can easily turn into a bitter, unforgiving and angry woman. Beware lest you lay down your armor! Remember what happened to David. He laid down his armor and blood and judgment were put upon his family.

**Don't Use Your Armor as a Barrier to Relationships**

Now, I've been telling you to use your armor and this may seem contradictory to you, but in using our armor for God, we can also get caught up in using our armor as a barrier to hide behind.

I remember a lady who always came to the women's Bible study at our church, and she was very hard to teach. My self-image told me that I wasn't good enough as a teacher and she didn't respond to my teaching. That's all I could see. I believed that she didn't like *me*, but that she came out of respect for the pastor—and all her friends came.

But that wasn't the case at all.

She was using her armor as a barrier to block me and everyone else out.

Because of my own insecurities, I couldn't see it nor get through it.

Eventually, this woman fell into sin, and left her husband and children. I was so convicted by the Holy Spirit for thinking of myself so much that I missed what was going on in her. What could I have done for her?

I realize that her own armor was her barrier, but if my armor had been on correctly, maybe I could have seen her need with accuracy and discernment. Instead, my armor covered my eyes so I couldn't see her need. I couldn't see beyond myself to help her.

Look at your armor. Is it so high that no one can get to you? Do you get mad at other Christians because you think, "no one likes me".

Someone told me once that the way I walk and the way I talk shows a person whether I am open to talk or not. There are times when I am on a mission and I don't want to talk. Sometimes that's bad. Sometimes that's good. My demeanor has a way of saying, *I've got to go accomplish something and I've got to do it now.*

There are other times when you are using your "armor" for the wrong purpose. When I don't know what to say or do, I put up my armor and use it to fend people off. I've had to determine when it's really the time to use my armor and when it's not.

Learn how to risk in relationships. Yes, some people may use you, abuse you, be mean to you, and gossip about you, but don't misuse your armor to keep others out. Let people into your life. God wants people to be a part of your life because they will help you get to your destiny.

Like David, know who you are and who you aren't.

Slay the giants from your past.

Deal a death blow to rejection, intimidation, and inferiority with the Word of God.

Replace Satan's thoughts with God's thoughts—and enjoy a new life of seeing yourself through God's eyes.

## Confess God's Word Over Yourself Today!

*God has set before me life and death...Today I choose life in all the words that I speak, and I will speak words of life and encouragement in everyone I meet. I think before I speak and I choose to understand before being understood. Wherever I go, the Spirit of God goes before me and when I enter a room, the atmosphere is charged with the love of God. I am a woman of integrity, and I speak the truth at all times. I follow through on everything that I say, and I bring to completion even the smallest of tasks. I am a trustworthy woman and I keep in confidence what others have confided in me. Today I choose character over personal gain, people over things, to serve over to gain power, my principles over convenience, and the long term over immediate gratification.*

*—Molly Venzke*

# Questions To Consider

1. What people and/or situations (giants) come up in your life that are intimidating you?

2. How can you use the Word to fight against the intimidation?

3. In what ways have you used your "armor" to keep people away?

4. Have you become lax in your Christian walk lately? What are you going to do today to make a change?

Caleb 10, Micah 6

*Sometimes you just
need a little help to make
the next step.*

# Chapter
## FIVE

### The Myth of Earning Acceptance
*And the truth about your appearance, performance and importance.*

In his book, *His Image, My Image*, Josh McDowell shares the story of what happened at the 1929 Rose Bowl Game. It's a great picture of how we cannot earn God's acceptance.

Two teams were at the Rose Bowl. One of the players picked up a fumbled play and began running. One of his teammates started to run after him. The other team didn't run at all. The first player thought he was running for the big touchdown, but he was running the wrong way, giving the opposing team a three-point touchback, which put the opposing team ahead.

At halftime, the teams went into their locker rooms, and the guy who ran the wrong way put his head in his lap and sobbed. He felt he had failed everyone. He said, "The highlight of our life is right here and I blew it." Everyone on his team felt totally depressed.

Then the coach made a surprising move. He said, "We're starting with the same players in the second half."

The guy blurted out, "I can't go."

The coach told him, "You have to go."

"But I have failed the team. I can't look at them. I can't look at the fans."

The coach responded, "You have to go back out there and do what I want you to do. I want you to play."

So the player went out and played harder than the coach had ever seen a team member play in his life.

Josh McDowell says that is just like God. In a situation where we have totally failed, and we can honestly look at the situation and say we have failed, God always extends forgiveness and gives us another chance.

And He'll do it for anyone.

Perhaps you've gone through a divorce and you have

*The more confident we are in God's loving gaze, the less driven we will be to win the loving gaze of others.*
*- Cynthia Hicks*

admitted that you were the cause of it. Maybe you committed adultery. You might even have children because of your adulterous affair or because of your immoral lifestyle before you were married. Whatever your failure is, you will always have to live with it, but rather than live condemned, you can live forgiven.

The man in the story had to live the

rest of his life with the fact that he ran the wrong way. He did something totally unacceptable, and he had to live with that fact. Yet, he was forgiven—and accepted.

## You Can't Earn God's Love

You can't earn God's forgiveness or His acceptance. But you can receive it. John 15:13 says, ***Greater love has no one than this, than to lay down one's life for his friends.***

God has commended His love toward us and for us. And there is no greater love than what Jesus has for us.

Yet, people keep trying to earn God's acceptance—as well as man's. They keep trying to get people and God to accept them and forgive them for their mistakes.

When you see a person who has made a major mistake, what do you do to that person?

Usually, you accept them, you forgive them, and you don't hold it against them. Usually, the only one we hold something against is ourselves.

Your acceptance is based on what God has done—not on what you have done.

But you—and most other people—don't act like that. You try to earn your rightful place in God's kingdom. You try to become a powerful person, instead of allowing yourself to be what God wants

*Darkness cannot drive out darkness; only light can do that. Hate cannot drive out hate; only love can do that.*
*- Martin Luther King, Jr.*

89

you to be.

Do you see the difference?

When you don't feel accepted, there's such a big difference in how you relate to people, how you talk to people, how you act around people. When you're trying all the time to be accepted, you'll do things that are goofy. You'll say things that aren't right. Out of insecurity or from a low self-image, you will try to look good. When you are supposed to be somewhere at a certain time and you are ten minutes late, out of a low self-image you will say the reason you're late is because you got caught in traffic, when the truth is, you got a late start.

In short, you make excuses for yourself. Or, you defend yourself.

How many times have you said, "You didn't treat me right"?

The real reason you're mad or defensive is because you have not accepted the love of God. You haven't accepted yourself in God. You still want to earn your place, not just from God, but from people.

To change, you'll have to do more than just say that you will see yourself and think of yourself as God thinks about you and sees you. You will also need to focus on not letting your thoughts steal, kill or destroy you. Determine in your heart, *I'm not going to allow those types of thoughts to control my life. I'm going to allow my thoughts to be centered on the abundance of what God has for me, on*

*His acceptance of me just as I am.*

God commended. He declared. He spoke. He said, "That's the way it is. My love is given."

You don't earn it. You can't.

When you're in the midst of a battle, that's when you need to stop and say, "Okay, I don't have to defend myself. I don't have to be a perfect person. I don't have to be the right one, because I am loved. I don't have to be anything except who God called me to be." And you are called to be a *child of the King.*

Romans 5:8 assures you of God's love:

**But God demonstrates His own love toward us, in that while we were still sinners, Christ died for us.**

When you're in the midst of sharing with a friend, or even counseling with her, you don't have to make things perfect. You don't have to do everything just right. When you are in a prayer group and you are asked to pray, your prayer doesn't have to be perfect. In fact, people don't dry up spiritually because they can't pray perfectly. They dry up because they do not feel accepted.

Humility is acceptance of the place annointed by God, whether it be in the front or in the rear.
- Charles Spurgeon

## Accept Yourself

God's grace says, "I love you."

His grace says, "I forgive you."

God's grace says, "You are My child."

His grace says, "Greater am I in you than he who is in the world. You are my shining light on this earth."

God's grace is not earned. God has given it. When you don't accept God's grace, you frustrate His grace.

For example, when you look in the mirror or when a situation arises and someone asks, "Can you help?" are some of your first thoughts...

- ❖ *I'm not capable.*
- ❖ *I'm not smart enough.*
- ❖ *I'm not good enough.*
- ❖ *Look at all the bad things I have done in the past.*
- ❖ *How can I counsel a person to love her children when I had an abortion?*
- ❖ *How can I counsel them to succeed in their marriage if I've had a divorce?*
- ❖ *How can I help a person love themselves when I've had trouble loving myself?*
- ❖ *How can I feel good about my body when I am not in shape?*

When these types of thoughts are allowed to come crashing into your brain, and you say, "No, I can't help," you frustrate the grace of God.

Were you forgiven?

If you haven't asked for forgiveness, then you need to. But if you have, then you are forgiven. So, receive it. Receive His grace and keep moving on.

Change comes with forgiveness and acceptance of yourself. When you receive your forgiveness, then you are operating in the grace of God. You are operating in the love of God, and you are not frustrating His grace.

The bottom line is, God's grace uses a bunch of hodgepodge people. The Body of Christ is made up of a "dirty dozen"! That's what we *were*—the cons of the cons, the dirtiest of the dirty, and the foulest of the foul. But, in His grace, we are unconditionally loved!

How can you not accept yourself when God accepts you?

So you did some terrible things. God still loves you. You must accept yourself. You must say, "Yes, I made some mistakes but I am accepted by God." You might have lost in a certain situation. You might have been responsible for something bad that happened. But you still have to go beyond that and accept the person God has chosen to love—YOU!

Paul allowed Stephen to be stoned to death at his feet. Though he allowed that to happen, he stood up later in his life and said he wronged no man (II Corinthians 7:2). How could he say that? He accepted God's forgiveness and grace.

## You Are Accepted in the Body of Christ

God has accepted you from before the foundation of the world. You are His creation. He loves you—and the "ways" that you are. He created your "bents" for His glory. He created you as a valuable part of the Body of Christ. Your input is required, desired and essential.

I know it sounds so simple to say, "Be a part of the Body of Christ." But it is true. God wants you active in the Body for your good, and the good of others.

The Bible says you are protected in the Body. You are protected by being a part of the Church. Every person has a part to play. Each of us fills a different role in the ministry. I need you and you need me. I need your input into my life.

Ephesians 4:16 says, ***From whom the whole body, joined and knit together by what every joint supplies, according to the effective working by which every part does its share, causes growth of the body for the edifying of itself in love.***

If my emotional tank is on empty, I need the Word of God to fill my tank, but I also need you. I need the Word of God to come through you. I need the love of God to come through you. I need the acceptance of God to come through you, because I cannot see God. I can only see Him in you, and I can feel Him working in you toward me. I need that acceptance from you to fill up my tank. When my tank gets full, then I am able to move again—and I am able to fill your tank so you can continue supplying other tanks.

It's a never-ending cycle of love and acceptance.

I John 4:11-12 makes it clear:

***Beloved, if God so loved us, we also ought to love one another. No one has seen God at any time. If we love one another, God abides in us, and His love has been perfected in us.***

If I don't know you and you don't know me, then how can we know the acceptance of God? How can we grow in knowing the love of God?

By actively being involved in the Body of believers.

It is critical that we meet regularly with other believers. Weekly Bible studies are so valuable. Church services with the whole family are so important! We are to stir one another up!

***And let us consider one another in order to stir up love and good works.*** *(Hebrews 10:24)*

All of us know Christians who were growing with God and doing things for God in the church, when suddenly they quit being involved. They became too busy with other things and had to quit different areas of church involvement. They are the ones you don't see anymore. And when you do talk to them, you sense an emptiness in them, and they talk about all the negative things happening in their lives.

When we gather in Christian settings, we need the comfort, the hugs and the ability to look each other in the face and say, "I'm glad you're here today."

We need the person who says, "You are so beautiful.

I'm so glad you're my friend."

We need those kinds of words that build us up. Of course, I'm not saying to build your self-image on what other people think, but I am saying you need to receive the love and acceptance of God through people.

What I am describing isn't living off the naturalness of man. It's living off how the Word comes out of you to me, and how the Word comes out of me to you.

It's the life flow that God wants in the Body of Christ. Hebrews 10:24-25 says it best: ***And let us consider one another in order to stir up love and good works, not forsaking the assembling of ourselves together, as is the manner of some, but exhorting one another, and so much the more as you see the Day approaching.***

The entire concept of Body life is to be linked together. That's what God intended. I need you and you need me. The things you do affect me in some way. In fact, as a member of the Body of Christ, everything you do affects me eventually. Your presence in my life, your prayers on the earth—they all affect me.

So, I need to accept God's love. I need to stay linked in the Body. I must be strong—and I draw strength from you and other believers.

In order to be the strong person God wants me to be, I must also be accountable. I must have a plan to have people in my life to whom I am accountable. Each of us needs to have accountability. We cannot be independent of one another.

No matter how hard you try, your own thinking will never get you out of the problems you face. You must get God's thinking to help you get out of the problems, because it is your own thinking that got you into the problems!

God uses other people to help you with your thinking. God uses everything and everyone from pastors, teachers, special friends, not-so-special friends, reading a book, reading the Bible, to watching Christian TV.

Your answers will come from the people who are around you. Balanced thinking will not come if you isolate yourself and seek your own desires. Proverbs 18:1 tells us: ***A man who isolates himself seeks his own desire; he rages against all wise judgment.***

You will rage against all wise judgment and wise input if you isolate yourself—whether you are around people or not.

It's easy to isolate yourself, yet live surrounded by people. It's a matter of vulnerability. It's a matter of the heart.

You are the only person who can open the door for others to come into your life and your heart. Your husband and your children can't. Your best friend can't. You are the only person with the key. God can't open the door to your heart and neither can the Holy Spirit.

Though He might be standing at the door of my heart

knocking, "Wendy, are you going to listen?" I can rage against all wise judgment—and rage doesn't mean loud yelling. It can mean that we turn a deaf ear to a person and not listen to wisdom.

When you have the opportunity to receive something from someone and you don't like it, your mind will begin to race and run with it. But what you are hearing may be the very thing that God is trying to say to you. So, don't rage within yourself and refuse to receive it. Open your heart to the message. Talk to God about it and allow people into your life.

God wants you to know that you are accepted and that you are unconditionally loved. You need to accept yourself and not frustrate God's grace that is working within you. He wants you to be a part of His Body and not be isolated from others. He doesn't want you to be by yourself. You are not an island. Be a part of what God is doing and allow yourself to grow up in Him.

## Develop An Accurate God View

By accepting God's love and grace, you can develop a more accurate God view of your image. I've said it before, but it bears repeating: you have to receive what God thinks about you over what people have said, over your thoughts of yourself, and over the devil's lies. You have to learn to look at yourself through God's eyes.

Your self-image is composed of conclusions you have

reached about yourself—the good and the not-so-good.

People with a poor self-image are not able to love and serve. They are tormented with ever-persistent questions:

"What am I going to get out of this?"

"What will they think about me?"

"How did I do?"

"What did I say?"

"How did I act?"

"Maybe I should, maybe I shouldn't."

That's why it is so important to rise up to a new level in Christ—no matter what condition your self-image is in right now. Go for more. Go for all the freedom Christ died to give you.

Whatever conclusions you have reached about yourself—up to this point in life—are mainly based on three primary areas in which you have judged yourself (many times this is how you judge others also). They are appearance, performance and importance.

**Of course, in today's society, *appearance* is the number one consideration.** It is amazing to me how focused we are on how we look. Bigger here, smaller there. The things that were beautiful a hundred years ago are not judged the same today. Can you imagine the plastic surgeons who would be out of work if they had been born 100 years ago? Liposuction would not have made it in the 1800's. Everything has changed.

And yet we judge so harshly on appearance. We decide

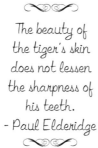

*The beauty of the tiger's skin does not lessen the sharpness of his teeth.*
*- Paul Elderidge*

how good we are or how important we are based on how we look—and how everyone else looks. We will never measure up to the person next door, and we will certainly never look like the girls on the magazine covers. *They* *don't even look like that in real life!*

It's funny and sad how we try so hard to be something that is next to impossible in the natural realm.

Is that really what we want?

Of course not.

**The second condition on which we judge** **ourselves so harshly is performance.** We are constantly checking on ourselves. *Am I okay? Am I good* *enough? Do I measure up? Am I creative enough? Am I* *okay as a wife or as a minister?*

Many times my emotions have been controlled by how I performed. If I feel I have performed well enough when teaching in a Bible study or a church service, then I have a great day. But, if I feel I rambled on or fumbled through the lesson, I tend to be depressed.

And that is just one small example of how many of us live our lives.

So often we judge ourselves on the here and now instead of on long-term performance. We don't remember the great thing we did yesterday to put it all in proper perspective. We are so willing and quick to put ourselves down based on how "we thought" we performed.

But that's a skewed perspective which leads to a poor self-image. When you feel badly about something, remember to look at what else you have done right. Look at the big picture, not just at one moment.

**The third condition by which we judge ourselves is importance.** The idea of "Am I important?" is a big area in dealing with self-esteem.

How many times have you been mentally bound by questions like:

"Who thinks I'm important?"

"Who doesn't think I'm important?"

"What do people say about me?"

"Why did they choose someone else to do that project?"

Ouch!

You can't live off of what people say about you. You have to get your feelings of importance and worth from God's Word. Let Him work within you, step-by-step, to be who He wants you to be.

Corrie ten Boom often showed a piece of embroidery to her audiences. She would hold up the piece of cloth, first showing the beauty of the embroidered side, with all the threads forming a beautiful picture, which she described as the plan God has for our lives. Then she would flip it over to show the tangled, confused, underside, illustrating how we view our lives from a human standpoint.
- Author Unknown

It is His process.

The truth is, regardless of how you feel, you are important in His plan. But, so often we try to get our importance by getting others to recognize who we are. Or, we try to get our feelings of importance by attaining certain levels of responsibility in different areas.

You have to overcome the myth that you can earn acceptance—by your appearance, your performance or your feelings of importance. In fact, the only way you will be able to "see" who you are in Christ is to get rid of those things pulling you down. You have to get rid of those things that continually stop you from moving forward in Christ!

## Confess God's Word Over Yourself Today!

*I am a happy and supportive wife. I am a safe place for my husband's dreams. I help cultivate and germinate my husband's goals and ideas. I do not make decisions based on fear, but on the wisdom of God. I am an active and patient mom. I am not lazy, but I am a warrior, guarding the hearts of my children. I am wise and Word-led in laying down my children's foundation. I am a true friend. I listen to the hearts of my friends. I have grace for their strengths and weaknesses. I am friendly and go out of my self to be friendly. I am honest and I only speak the truth. I have a heart after God. I desire to know Him as a friend who speaks to a friend. I desire to know all His goodness, not out of my need, but to know Him better. I desire to know His voice and I am faithful and disciplined to listen. I am not too busy for God, but I am busy for God. I am moved with compassion and not my own selfish agenda.*

*—Jill Cooper*

# Questions To Consider

1. Are there situations in your life where you know that you have failed? Write down one incident or situation.

2. Think about how God's love covers over a multitude of sin. Can you see how God's love can cover (forgive) in your situation? If you haven't yet, ask God to forgive you and let it go. Spend some time thanking God for forgiveness and healing in this situation.

3. Look up and write out three scriptures on love and/ or forgiveness.

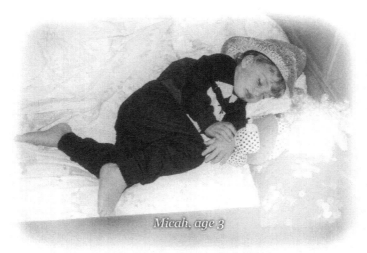

Micah, age 3

*I'm getting up now...ZZZZZ...*
*Ok, I'm getting up <u>now</u>...zzzz...OK <u>NOW</u>...*

# Chapter
## SIX

## What Really Keeps You From Changing
*Even when you say you want to.*


So what keeps you from changing the things you want changed? What's holding you back? You say you want to change—but you're not really motivated. I believe this chapter will help you identify what has been holding you back.

The devil has used many devices to destroy your self-image bit by bit over the years. To dismantle the strongholds to which you have become accustomed, you will need to identify them.

To help you, consider the following illustration:

Spiders anchor their webs with anchor lines to the surfaces of where they want their web to be attached. These anchor lines are like the areas in which we have a poor self-image or low self-esteem. These are the strongholds that have deep roots within us.

Once a spider has his anchor lines established, he builds

his web around them. Once the web is built, it "catches" flies, other insects and debris. The spider focuses on what has been caught in his web. He gives all his attention to the things which are caught because that is his sustenence.

You are like the spider.

You have anchors in your life that constantly cause you to feel down. You don't always recognize why because you are so busy continuing to build your web—and then things get caught.

For example, you're not really angry at that driver for pulling out in front of you. It's just a little bug that got caught in your web, so you honk at it. The driver is not really the problem. It's just a symptom of what is in your heart.

In your life, you have built a web in which things are constantly being caught, and you focus all of your attention chasing after the bugs rather than dealing with the anchors.

*You can't have a better tomorrow if you are thinking about yesterday all the time.*
*-Charles F. Kettering*

The reason you chase bugs and don't deal with your anchors is because removing the anchors hurts. So you go on with life, day after day, ignoring your anchors.

A poor self-image and low self-esteem will always cause you to hurt. As a result, you will run away from the things that hurt and go back to your web

108

because the web feels safer. So you deal with the small irritating things that happen to you, yet never deal with the true issues of your heart.

To pull up those anchors, and to develop a right self-image, you will have to trust someone to get some of the issues out in the open.

Unfortunately, if you are like many people, you haven't developed your trust in other people. You can be around people for ten years and still not trust them. You have to make the conscious decision to step out and say, "I will trust you."

"But I've been hurt," you say.

Yes, you've been hurt. Everyone has. Sometimes we think we're the only ones who have ever been hurt. We're the only ones who have ever experienced meanness, cruelty, or unkindness. Each one of us can give an account of some cruel act that was done to us. Some things were done on purpose and some were not.

But it's time to acknowledge it and remember that we are looking at those acts through our own perception. Sometimes we put too much emphasis on the things that are done to us, and we use that to shut people out of our lives.

In order to deal with your anchors, you have to trust someone with your emotions. Of course, it's easier to ignore

> Nobody gets
> to live life
> backward.
> Look ahead -
> that's where
> your future is.
> - Ann Landers

them, and run and maintain the web for the rest of your life. But, in maintaining the web, you're never free.

> The trouble with most of us is that we would rather be ruined by praise than saved by criticism.
> - Norman Vincent Peale

Just as when you have a spider web in your home, you can sweep the spider out his web, but if you leave him sitting there, all you did was deal with the symptoms. Soon the web will be re-built again.

So often it's easier to just deal with the web. Getting rid of the anchors is much more difficult. But pulling up the anchors and being willing to trust others to help you is the key to freedom.

It's a step of faith. And it's a journey.

## The Anchors of Low Self-Esteem

Once you have decided you want to pull up the anchors that have been holding you back...what do you do? First, you have to clearly identify what these are in your life. If you don't identify the specific anchors holding you down, you will never be able to pull them up.

To help you, I have compiled a list of some thoughts and attitudes that could be "anchors" in your life. This list is by no means complete, but just a starting point to try and stir up your thinking.

If you find yourself in several of these categories, don't

overreact. Simply use this as a tool to identify possible anchors.

- ❖ Thinking that God is not interested in you or that He is angry with you.
- ❖ Self-conscious about your appearance, or performance.
- ❖ A competitive view of others as people to conquer, not friends to enjoy.
- ❖ Striving to become something or somebody, instead of relaxing and enjoying who you are.
- ❖ Very sensitive to the opinions of others.
- ❖ A need for flattery or to be admired.
- ❖ Living in the past or future, rather than the present.
- ❖ Always wondering what other people meant.
- ❖ Always seeing the glass half empty, instead of half full.
- ❖ Feeling insecure in social situations.
- ❖ Always ready to criticize and see the worst in others.
- ❖ Defensive in behavior and conversation, "Carrying a chip on your shoulder."
- ❖ A tendency to have your "one best friend."
- ❖ Not able to readily receive compliments.
- ❖ Letting others walk on you.
- ❖ Mentally re-thinking past conversations or situations without solving them.
- ❖ Negative self-talk. Putting yourself down and saying things like, "I can't believe I did that!"
- ❖ Always expecting the worst to happen to you.
- ❖ Need for material possessions to insure a feeling of security or to impress others.
- ❖ A need to make sure everything is "perfect".
- ❖ Inability to take responsibility for negative situations or feelings.
- ❖ Need for lots of structure and controlling behavior.

Many of us run from really taking a look at these things, but you cannot conquer something by running from it. You have to face them and begin to see what needs to be pulled up in your life.

Did you see more than one anchor that has been holding you down? Now that you are aware you can begin to pull these up and start the process of change. Awareness is the first step to freedom.

## Anchors that will keep you stuck

There are so many things the devil can use in our lives to keep us from changing.

*Sometimes it is a lack of knowing what to change.* Sometimes we just don't see the need to change. Or we just seem to get stuck in a rut and everything stays the same. How many times have you said, "I need to change that!" only to say the same thing again next week? It's the perpetual "New Year's resolution."

*Sometimes people don't go for change because they are comfortable with things the way they are.*

You might not like every detail of your life, but it's comfortable. It's comfortable to be around the same people and act the same way you always do. People expect you to act that way. You don't even have to think about it. You don't have to challenge yourself. The people who are around you are comfortable with the way you act. You don't challenge them and they don't challenge you.

It's a nice arrangement.

You can become so comfortable that you don't try to make changes. Consider your financial situation. Yes, you want prosperity, but it becomes comfortable not having enough. You've lived with the feeling of lack so long that the idea of pressing into God for your needs or in finding a better job is more uncomfortable than the stress of not paying your bills.

Why is it that people who make a certain income and then double their income, soon find themselves in the same pressure situation of not having enough? Because they tend to rise to their place of comfort and live in that.

And that's why you have not changed things about yourself. You are comfortable.

## No Guts, No Glory

*Maybe the anchor holding you down is a lack of guts.* The lack of determination to attack a problem will keep you from changing. If you don't have the attitude that you're so fed up with the condition of your life that you'll do whatever it takes to change it, you won't. It takes fortitude, strength and guts to say, "I'm not going to put up with this anymore. I am going to attack it with everything that is within me."

Conforming to the image of Christ takes guts. It takes work. If you don't think it is work, then you haven't attacked anything. I can guarantee you there are challenges that will continue to attack you unless you determine within yourself to overcome them.

You will have temptations come back repeatedly until you're determined to rid yourself of them. It will be subtle at first. You'll refuse, but after a while you will be lulled back into that thought pattern or behavior. You won't consciously think about it, but you will need the guts to stand up to any opposition to God's will for your life.

And you'll always be tempted the most when you are alone. That's why I believe being connected to the Body of Christ is so important to your success. It protects you, because temptation won't succeed in the company of strong friends. The devil will wait until you're alone to get you to think his way.

## Patience Is Required

*Maybe your anchor is impatience.* How many times have you said, "I've been trying to get rid of this thing for two weeks now"?

Excuse me. You might as well know from the very beginning that you won't overcome everything in one day. You won't overcome everything in two days, a month, or a year. It is only through faith and patience that you inherit the promises of God (Hebrews 6:12).

For example, when you forgive someone for a situation that has a lot of depth and pain, you can't expect it to just disappear. You forgave by choice, but many times you do not have an emotional feeling of freedom when you forgive.

I remember a situation which took me four and a half years before my choice to forgive changed into the *feeling* of forgiveness. But I never gave up. I had forgiven by choice, but the scar of it was still there for a long time.

Some wounds are deeper than others. How many times have you heard, "Forgive and forget"? We tend to think all the thoughts and feelings are totally gone as soon as we have made the decision to forgive. We know that's not really true.

I was hit by a car when I was younger and have two major scars on my leg. I don't think about the scars. They do not hurt me. I could not pick at the scar and open the wound back up, but just the same, the scar is there. It did not just disappear from my memory. It's still there, though it does not hurt anymore.

In changing and growing, the reality is, there are certain things we will never forget. They are merely scars that no longer hurt. They do not have the power to hurt us anymore because we have chosen to let them go.

You need to resist doubt. Faith and patience are required in fighting for change. You want action now. You want it to change now. But some things take time to heal and change. Allow that process to happen within you. At the same time be persistent to make a change. Dwell on the positive.

## I'm OK, You're OK

*Maybe your anchor is simply that you truly believe, "I'm OK, so why should I change?"*

For example, you may observe your family, see certain weaknesses, but settle for the same by telling yourself, "I turned out OK."

If you justify your choices this way, you are lacking the drive to change. You do not see there could be a better future for yourself and your children. And you're living in denial.

The truth is that you probably did turn out OK because of God's grace. Someone may have prayed for you and God just helped you out.

Rather than face the truth, you put on your rose-colored glasses, look at your past, and say, "Oh, wasn't that wonderful?" when in reality, there were a lot of negative things that have affected how you live your life now.

It's understandable that you want to look at yourself and say, "Hey, I'm not too bad."

I know I've had to meditate on this in my life because I have a tendency to say, "Hey, everything's cool."

When I look at my family, I see that my brothers and sisters all love God, but some of us don't have a really great relationship with one another. A few of us do, but it's not like we grew up with really close relationships. If I didn't see that as a hindrance in my life, I would not know to train my children differently. I'd continue to believe "Everything's fine, I'm happy, I've got friends, I'm normal," instead of, "Wait a minute. Everything wasn't perfect back then."

Facing the truth is a vital step to changing your self-image into the image of Christ.

I'm not saying that you should condemn your parents. But I am saying you need to face the truth and see what can change accordingly. It will make a difference in how your raise your children and you will pass on something better to the next generation.

Personally, I'm amazed at some of the ways we allow our parents to control our adult lives. Even though we are tormented with negative thoughts, and feelings of inadequacy from childhood, what do we do? We place our children into the primary place we received our training!

Many of our children spend weeks and weekends with our parents on a regular basis. Unless there has been some radical change in that home, why are we allowing negativity to be sown into the hearts of our kids? Why do we sit by quietly while letting negative family members take control and speak contrary to the Word of God over our children?

Why are you so drawn to the past? Why do you find yourself doing the same things that you disagree with your parents, your sisters, or your brothers about? Why do you keep repeating the same old habits?

It's because you are comfortable with the "status quo".

I'm not trying to knock your family, because I don't believe in blaming your past for who you are today. However, I do think you need to have a clear vision of your past. Most of us don't have as clear of a vision as we think we do. An anchor of "the familiar ways" keep us from changing because it's comfortable, and we like things the way they are.

Dare to break out! Dare to challenge the familiar ways. Dare to change for yourself—and for your children.

### You Need A Map

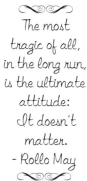

*The most tragic of all, in the long run, is the ultimate attitude: It doesn't matter.*
*- Rollo May*

***Another anchor that might be holding you back is a lack of definite goals and direction.***

Why are you not progressing in life, in your spirit, in your emotions, in your finances, in your socializing and in the physical arena? More than likely it is because you lack defined goals. You mumble and grumble through life and that's all you do. You have a lot of ideas, but you do not really know where you are going in life.

What are your goals for your family? What are your goals for your finances? Why do you spend certain hours *with* your children and certain hours *away* from them?

At Christian Faith Center, where Casey and I pastor, many women are faithful to the Wordshop, our women's

Bible study, every week but others only come occasionally. If a woman has a definite goal of *why* she attends Wordshop, she never misses.

When you have a definite goal of why you participate in something, you always make it happen. If you do not have a definite goal, you will just show up when it's convenient, or when it works with your schedule. You will simply sleepwalk through life—and miss what's most important.

Do you have definite financial goals? Definite social goals?

If you don't have any definite goals, then why work on yourself? You are comfortable to go through life accepting the status quo—just living a good life, but not the best life.

But life is about so much more.

Think about all of the lost people around you who happen to be good people. They are bound for hell because goodness does not save anyone. According to Ephesians 2:8-9, it requires faith: ***For by grace you have been saved through faith, and that not of yourselves; it is the gift of God, not of works, lest anyone should boast.***

Thousands of good people are settling for "a good life," but they are missing out on God's best life. Eternal life is achieved by faith in God. The best earth life is achieved by having goals and renewing the spirit of your mind to

119

conform to the image of Christ. It is achieved by having goals that move you towards becoming all that you were created to be—so you can fulfill your destiny.

## The Crippling Effects of Hurt

***Another anchor that can keep you from changing your self-image is hurt.*** Many times your image has been shaped by your past hurts. As you have taken hold of those hurts, your self-image has developed around them.

You have allowed your reaction to hurt to form your self-image and control your behavior and beliefs—for years.

No matter how old we get, we keep the negative images that were imprinted upon us years earlier. Some started out at a very young age with distorted ideas of who they are supposed to be. On top of that, they grow up getting even more distorted ideas from the world's point of view of how they should be.

Our distorted ideas can affect every area of our lives. For example, if you have ever been overweight and then lost weight, it's interesting to see what you still think about yourself.

I've had to deal with this. If I see someone to whom I've given clothes, I think, "They really look good in that". But I never thought that about myself when I wore it. I saw myself as much bigger. My viewpoint was distorted.

Usually the perception you and I have of ourselves is deceptive. We don't see a kind, thoughtful, patient, considerate, disciplined person.

Instead we relate if someone says, *lazy, impatient, irresponsible, slow, stupid, or bossy.*

We respond easily to the negative image because our view has been so distorted by the devil's point of view. The devil wants you to have a poor self-image, because when you have a poor self-image, you do not aggressively do all God has placed within you. You live in a small world thinking only of yourself and all of your limitations. You are consumed with your inabilities—or what you *perceive* to be your inabilities.

But with a right self-image—with knowing who you are—you don't think about yourself. You look at yourself through God's eyes and then think about others. Your mind becomes set on how to help other people, how to love and give to them.

Josh McDowell also wrote in his book, *His Image, My Image,* "What is self-worth? *The absence of concentration upon yourself.* It means that while I like and accept myself, I don't need to prove my worth excessively either to myself or to others." (p. 42-43)

That is a strong self-image.

I used to want to be like Marilyn

Now's the time to reach the goals, now's the time to stand and fight.
- Peter Daniels

Hickey. I wanted to be a world-wide preacher. As I've learned to accept myself, I no longer need to prove my worth or my abilities to others. And with my sense of worth has come the realization that I don't want to be like Marilyn Hickey anymore. She has her job, and I have mine!

Personally, I've grown in knowing who I am in Christ. I have developed confidence in Wendy Treat, as a daughter of my loving Heavenly Father. Basically that's it. I used to need to add on the other things I do, but as I've grown in knowledge, I have found that everything else is no longer important.

In the past, I needed to prove how valuable I was. I wanted to do all these important things and make sure everybody honored me, but I've continued growing and conforming my image to that of Jesus Christ. And because of Him, I have found that I can think so much more about other people, about Casey, and about my children, instead of worrying about myself.

I don't live out of past hurts. I live out of who I am in Christ. I live seeing myself through God's eyes.

## Forgiveness Leads to Freedom

Remember, growth is a step-by-step process. I don't expect you to do everything in this book perfectly and be a clone. The Word of truth has to be developed within you.

Just keep God's standard in the forefront of your thinking:

*Finally, brethren, whatever things are true, whatever things are noble, whatever things are just, whatever things are pure, whatever things are lovely, whatever things are of good report, if there is any virtue and if there is anything praiseworthy – meditate on these things.* (Philippians 4:8)

And in your behavior:

*Love is patient, love is kind. It does not envy, it does not boast, it is not proud. It is not rude, it is not self-seeking, it is not easily angered, it keeps no record of wrongs. Love does not delight in evil but rejoices with the truth. It always protects, always trusts, always hopes, always perseveres. Love never fails.* (I Corinthians 13:4-8, NIV)

How many wrongs do you remember?

I realize that some people have had horrible things happen to them. For me to say to you, "Just forget the wrongs," you would probably respond, "She doesn't know what she's talking about. She doesn't even know how badly I was hurt."

You're right. I don't know. But I do know you are no different than anyone else. No matter the depth of your hurt you need to forgive the wrongs done to you. In order for you to be set free and walk in the fullness of God's image on this earth, *you must let go of the past and take hold of today!*

It will be hard at times, but you *can* turn your past around. If you have always looked at things as half empty, you have seen yourself as not capable, you have heard it said that you're ugly, you will show that image to those around you. If that's the image you keep showing, that's the image that will keep coming back to you. We live in a mirrored environment. What you give is what you get, because that is what you see. You blind yourself to the positive.

In dealing with self-image, I'm trying to paint a picture in your mind so that when you are considering negative thoughts, the Word will come back to your mind. When you are feeling bad, you can decide, *I will think God-thoughts about myself.* When you want to think wrong about yourself, suddenly the Word, which is God's image that you are conforming to, causes you to think correctly. Instead you will think on just, pure and lovely things.

## How You Think Is How You Will Act

You will act the way you think.

If you think evil, you will act that way.

If you think of yourself as impatient, fat, ugly and undisciplined, guess what?

Out of the abundance of your heart, not only will your mouth speak, but you will act. If you believe it doesn't hurt for you to think of yourself that way, you are wrong.

When you believe wrong thoughts about yourself, the evil you believe will stop you from doing anything to meet the needs of the people around you. Even worse, when you allow those thoughts to control you, you are keeping others from the God in you, the hope of glory.

If you are in the right cycle, it's a wonderful, victorious cycle. You will catch yourself thinking a bad thought, stop and decide you love people too much to think that way. You will start thinking God's thoughts: "I am a patient, trusting, loving, and kind woman of God." As you begin to think and speak about yourself, you will begin to act that way to the people around you. That's what will come forth out of you, because that's what you perceive about yourself (Romans 4:17b).

Remember the quote from Josh McDowell? "While I like and accept

*Life is a grindstone. Whether it grinds you down or polishes you up depends upon what you are made of.*
*- Author Unknown*

myself, I don't need to prove my worth excessively either to myself or to others." I don't need to prove to you that I am thoughtful. I don't need to prove to you that I am patient. I don't have to prove to you that I'm not rude. I just need to be.

BE!

Be a happy person. When you take a look at yourself through God's eyes, you will portray the image of God to yourself and those around you. Be the image of God on this earth.

# Confess God's Word Over Yourself Today!

*I will smile today because this is the day my God has made. I am God's creation and He has already made a place for me in His church. Each day I discover my destiny and live the life He has prearranged for me. I hear God's voice and trust Him so I obey His Words. My husband and I walk hand-in-hand all the days of our life. I am an honorable wife and I keep no record of wrong. I have healthy, obedient kids. I am a patient mom, full of creativity. I see the gifts in my children and raise them according to their God-given capacity. My businesses are prosperous and influential. I see opportunities and follow through on God ideas. I am friendly and my home is welcoming; it is a gathering place for friends and family. I receive and extend grace. I embrace wisdom and seek understanding and let her promote me. I am protected from all harm or sickness because I dwell in the secret place of the Most High.*

*—Tina Scott*

# Questions To Consider

1. Write down one of the areas that keeps you from changing.

2. Explain how this holds you back from changing. Give specific examples.

3. What can you do to overcome in this area? Ask your mate or a close, godly friend to help you be accountable to work on this area of change.

Micah, age 5

*I thought this would be easier,*
*but hey, let's try it again!*

# Chapter
## SEVEN

### How Your Right Self-Image Will Propel You
*You'll finally walk beyond your experience and into your destiny.*

When you develop a right self-image, you will see yourself as God sees you—no more and no less. You will have arrived at having right vision and perception. How you see yourself will no longer be skewed by past experience, pain, fear and all of the negative words ever spoken over you. In short, you'll experience reality in God, which will propel you into your destiny.

Your destiny is to fulfill the call of God on your life with total abandonment and trust in God. It is the most freeing place to live in the universe.

In this place you will live in total freedom to be and do all that you were created to do...things you will "naturally" love because they are who you really are. What you will like, desire and experience will be what you've always wanted...and they will be the desires God has placed within your being.

Philippians 2:13 says, ***For it is God who works in you both to will and to do for His good pleasure.***

What an amazing cycle of freedom! What He begins in you, He will complete.

***Being confident of this very thing, that He who has begun a good work in you will complete it until the day of Jesus Christ.*** *(Philippians 1:6)*

Since before you were born, God has had an awesome plan for your life. That plan is your destiny. Even now, He wants you to have a sense of it. He wants you to know it. It's not a secret. He's called you as a mighty woman of valor, as an individual, and as a cherished daughter. He is eager to talk to you.

Jeremiah 1:5 says, ***Before I formed you in the womb I knew you; before you were born I sanctified you; I ordained you a prophet to the nations.***

In this verse, God was speaking to Jeremiah about his destiny.

Jeremiah responded, ***Ah, Lord GOD! Behold, I cannot speak, for I am a youth*** (verse 6).

You might be responding to God right now—even after reading this book—saying, "I'm not educated. I'm dumb, busy, afraid, young, shy, old or plain. I'm a woman. I'm black. I'm white. I'm Asian."

If so, you sound like Jeremiah: *For I am a youth.*

Just like Jeremiah, God wants you to go beyond your experience. He knew who you were and He formed you

132

before your parents even thought about you. God knew you before you were born, even if you were adopted. He is the One who made the plans for your life—and for Jeremiah's.

Here's the rest of the story. God didn't let Jeremiah off the hook...

> *But the Lord said to me: "Do not say, 'I am a youth,' for you shall go to all to whom I send you, and whatever I command you, you shall speak. 'Do not be afraid of their faces, for I am with you to deliver you,' says the Lord. Then the Lord put forth His hand and touched my mouth, and the Lord said to me: 'Behold, I have put My words in your mouth.' See, I have this day set you over the nations and over the kingdoms, to root out and to pull down, to destroy and to throw down, to build and to plant.*
> *(Jeremiah 1:7-10)*

And God won't let you off the hook either. He loves you! He's promised the same thing to you that He promised to Jeremiah. You have been individually called. God knows you. He formed you, ordained you and He touched you. Don't be a victim any longer. Rise up to the occasion to which God has called

*I am only one; but still I am one. I cannot do everything, but still I can do something. I will not refuse to do the something I can do.*
*- Helen Keller*

133

you.

What is your destiny? What are you to do in this life? There's a destiny for your life to which God has called you that you are to fulfill—and then there are destinies for the different seasons in your life you are to fulfill.

But for each season, you must get with God to ask Him what His plan and purpose is for your life right now.

## He Has a Destiny for Every Season of Life

Throughout the seasons of life, God will give you the destiny and purpose for each and every season, if you ask Him. Your destiny in one season, will propel you to the next. That is because during one season He will work with you and develop in you the ability to move to the next. He will continuously work with you as you seek His face.

> The important thing to remember is that if you don't have that inspired enthusiasm that is contagious whatever you do have is also contagious
> - Danny Cox

As I mentioned earlier, for a specific season of time a lot of my personal destiny was centered around rearing my children. Though, as a minister, I was still called to influence nations, my destiny, purpose and focus was centered on my three children. My destiny was to train and teach them and keep them focused on the will of God. I focused on being the kind of mother God wanted me to be, to be an example to my children,

134

to allow them to walk after me and after Christ. That was very strong in my life during that season.

Part of my personal destiny has always been to be the best wife I can be, to help and encourage my husband. God knew before the earth was founded that I was going to be married to Casey and have three children. That is a huge part of the destiny of my life, and it is very important.

In the same way, you have a personal destiny in your life. Your personal destiny isn't to "win the world" all the time. It's to hear God for the priority of today.

## Lay Hold of Your Personal Destiny

Whatever your destiny is for today, don't walk away from it. Walk toward it. If it is to be a wife, a mother, a friend, recognize how critical it is to fulfill that destiny. You have the power to affect generations! Don't belittle your calling. It's big, big, big! Galatians 3:29 tells you how big your calling really is: ***And if you are Christ's, then you are Abraham's seed, and heirs according to the promise.*** That's who you are. If more people understood their destinies, our world would not be in the state it is in today.

Your destiny is not independent of others, but it is linked to others. For example, today there are people in my life helping me reach the destiny to which God has called me. Many people have helped me to reach where I am today by their encouragement, words, and help.

135

Today, I have more gratitude toward the people who helped me in my past—the pastors, teachers, friends and family—and instead of waiting, I want to recognize it now and have a heart of gratitude for those people who are in my life today.

*Champions are a rare breed. They trust God while others ask for answers. They step forward while everyone else prays for volunteers. They see beyond the dangers, the risks, the obstacles and the hardships.*
*- Lester Sumrall*

I have a heart of gratitude toward them and they have a heart of gratitude toward me. It's a two-way street. My gratitude comes out of the reality and knowledge that I am not independent of people. I need people and people need me.

Consequently, I know that in the future, God will bring more people into my life to help me press toward the mark of my destiny.

Recognize this in your own life. People are put into your life to help you fulfill God's plan. You are also put into people's lives to help them. You are just as valuable in the lives of others as they are in yours. We are not independent of each other.

Don't get your destiny so spiritually out of whack that you can't see it! Learn how to walk and fulfill your destiny. I have been walking in the plans and purposes of God's will for my life since I was formed in my mother's womb. I am not living a life of mistakes.

> ***The Lord has called Me from the womb; from the matrix of My mother He has made mention of My name...And now the Lord says, who formed Me from the womb to be His servant.***
> *(Isaiah 49:1,5)*

There is such a security in knowing you are supposed to be who you are. I love knowing that *God planned me. He wants me. I am here for Him. I am here to be His servant.* That fills my heart with, "I am loved, I am wanted, and I am known."

You are not here by error or accident. You might have gone through some very hellish situations that God didn't want for you. But, He knew you would go through that, and He has made a way to bring forth healing and restoration in your life. The truth is, He has called you to be His child, His servant and His ambassador on this earth.

*You just can't beat the person who never gives up.*
*- Babe Ruth*

## It's Your Choice

God wants you to be a mighty champion on this earth. He desires for you to grow and be equipped to stand against the ways of the devil. You will determine whether or not that will happen. It is up to you whether you will fulfill the destiny to which God has called you. It is so much easier to submit to His Holy Spirit, and to get the revelation of God to live a life of victory.

I love my life, my family, and my friends. I love the joy of the Lord that we can share. But it's all based upon choice. You can choose right or wrong. You can fulfill your destiny and purpose or give it up.

I beseech you to never give up. Never choose to rage against all wise judgment and teaching. Instead, submit to God's plans and purposes for your life. Then you will live the best life you could ever have! You will fulfill your destiny.

## Confess God's Word Over Yourself Today!

*Father, I thank You that your Word is truth, and as I know the truth, it will make me free. Everyday, I give my attention to Your Words and put Your Word before me at all times. I meditate on it to keep it in the midst of my heart and as I do this, Your Word brings life and health to all my flesh. I thank You for Your exceedingly great and precious promises. As I exercise faith and patience, I will inherit those promises. I choose to side with Your Word and not my circumstances. Thank You for providing everything I need in this life. I am fully persuaded that what You've promised You will perform for it is impossible for You to lie. So I stagger not at the promise of God, but am strengthened in faith as I give You all the glory.*

*—Cindy Ostrom*

# Questions To Consider

1. Write a list of your current priorities:

2. What are some areas of your list that you may need to reconsider?

3. Take some time right now to ask God how the above areas fit into your "destiny" priority list. Talk with your spouse and close friends also. If needed, make any changes in your schedule. (This could be to add in something you should be doing or taking off something you should not be doing at this time.)

*Caleb, age 5*

*What?*
*This isn't how you walk across the bridge?*

# Chapter
## EIGHT

## Change Happens Step by Step
*Through the power of faith.*

Changing your poor self-image into a right self-image is a step-by-step process. As you mature, more areas will become apparent that need growth. It's a process. As you act in obedience to the next step that God shows you, He will continue to help you mature.

For example, God may show you a weak area in your life where you need to grow. It may take one year, or maybe five years before you conquer that weakness.

That's OK, because in the process you will mature, grow stronger, become more knowledgeable of the Word, and build more stable, godly relationships. And once you do begin to feel you can walk in victory in that area, He'll take you to the next area of growth.

Growing in Christ isn't always in leaps and bounds. Sure you want God to change you NOW! But there is a process of growing in the Word of God. That is how God works—through a process He calls seedtime and harvest.

Consider a seed that is planted. In the natural realm, if you are going to grow zucchini, you have to plant a zucchini seed. Once the seed is in the ground, you don't see it, or any manifestation of it. But as you water it, and the sun shines on it day by day, suddenly a little shoot will come up through the soil. That shoot will keep growing until it eventually becomes a very large plant, which produces a harvest of zucchini.

That's what happens within us, too. As we learn a principle of God's Word, it is like seed planted in our heart. It's not going to grow to maturity immediately. It will take some time.

As you take the truths presented in this book, and plant them like seeds in your heart, as you use your faith, they will grow—and you will change.

*Quality is never an accident, it represents the wise choice of many alternatives.*
*- Willa A. Foster*

Don't be concerned in the seasons when you aren't "seeing" the growth. It's happening even if you don't see it. Continue to feed your spirit man. In times like that, look at where you've been. Look at what God has done. Think about yourself five, ten, or even 15 years ago. Think about what you were afraid of and what you thought of others. You will probably see great growth has occurred.

Often we see so much growth in others around us, but we see none in ourselves—because we are preoccupied with our own needs. We fail to see reality because of our poor self-image.

Having the right self-image is critical to your success in life. Changing from how you see yourself now, to how God sees you is a process of change that requires your faith. You choose to believe who the Word says you are by faith; believe that's who you are, and receive the truth.

And one day, you'll realize your thinking and perceptions have been changed...because your beliefs have changed.

Remember, to develop a right self-image requires knowing and believing who you are in Christ. And it requires using your faith to believe who you really are. By using both the Word and your faith together, you are not building a self-image according to the world. You are building it based upon God's Word. When you base your self-image on the Word of God, you won't do everything the world says to do.

Using your faith will be essential. Overcoming all of your old habits, emotional patterns, and wrong beliefs won't always be easy. You need to draw upon your faith to win and to change.

Remember Hebrews 11:6: ***But without faith it is impossible to please Him, for he who comes to God must believe that He is, and that He is a rewarder of those who diligently seek Him.***

You will have to call those things that are not happening in your life right now as though they are.

*While we do not look at the things which are seen, but at the things which are not seen. For the things which are seen are temporary, but the things which are not seen are eternal.*

(II Corinthians 4:18)

There is a difference between faking and walking by faith. Faking is pretending and ignoring what is really happening in your life. Walking by faith is recognizing the reality of that with which you are challenged, but attacking it and overcoming it with the Word.

Overcoming old patterns is not fighting on a natural battleground. It's not overcoming on your own. Maybe you've gone to all the self-esteem seminars, you've read all the self-esteem books, you've done everything in the natural to get yourself thinking right and feeling right.

But you haven't succeeded.

That's because true success is based upon knowing who you are in Christ, using your faith and asking God for help.

So do it. Look at yourself and what you want to change. Begin to release your faith by saying, "I'm going to use my faith. I call those things that be not as though they are. I walk in the spirit. I do not fulfill the lusts of my flesh. I yield to peace, joy, kindness, love, gentleness, truthfulness and patience. I am a faithful Christian."

Be encouraged. Some of the things you need to change will not be a part of you forever. They are not eternal.

For example, fear is not eternal. Self-doubt is not eternal. Worry is not eternal. Anger is not eternal.

The things that are eternal include love, peace, joy and kindness. As you begin to call yourself what the Word says about you, doubt will attack. But you attack back.

If you are attacked with timidity and think: *how can I speak it if I can't see myself as bold?* That is when you need to call those things that are not as though they are.

When you begin to call those things that "be not" as though they are, you are putting your faith into motion. It's a spiritual dynamic that goes to work for you. Faith begins to go into operation. As you use your faith toward the things inside of you, and not just the things on the outside of you, you'll begin to feel and know a sense of overcoming strength.

Suppose you've been saying that you're a woman who has a disciplined mind: "I walk in confidence and boldness." If there is a situation that you are totally fearful of—maybe it's simply that you have the opportunity to witness about Christ—speak courage into your life. Then, when you face the opportunity to witness, courage will come forth.

It is a step-by-step process. You say it and then you act on it. The first time you say it, it's not strong. The second time is better, the third is stronger, but by the sixth or seventh time, you're saying, *Glory to God! God lives big within me!* You get stronger every step of the way as you keep calling those things that are not as though they are, and then act on that confession.

## Be Gracious to Yourself

As you walk through the process of change—going from a poor self-image to a right one—take the time limits off the process. Be gracious to yourself. Generally speaking, we are people who want things done right now. Personally, I want myself glorified and holy and I want to be the best example to the whole world right now! But change in God is a step-by-step process.

So how much time does just one step take?

I don't know. The first step could take three months, but the second and the third only one month. How do we know? Suddenly you're on the fifth step and you're saying, come on! A month goes by, a year goes by, and suddenly the sixth, seventh, eighth, ninth, tenth, and eleventh steps are all behind you.

> *It is a mistake to look too far ahead. Only one link in the chain of destiny can be handled at a time.*
> *- Winston Churchill*

I do not know how it all works. That's why you have to put the Word of God into yourself constantly. Faith comes by *hearing* the Word, not by *having* heard the Word (Romans 10:17). You must hear the Word every day. So get tapes and books and go to Bible studies. Let yourself be fed the Word of God on a

148

continual basis.

As you hear the Word of God over and over, guard yourself against getting an "attitude," which is a hardness of the heart.

A person with hardness of the heart will say, *I've heard this before. I know that scripture.* Guard yourself against this destructive trap. It will sabotage your growth.

A person told me one time that once you've heard the message of salvation, you don't need to hear it again. That's not true. Every time I hear the message of salvation, I receive more revelation of who I am in Christ. I receive more revelation of what salvation means. I receive more revelation that I am saved by grace.

You can't stop listening to the Word. When you've heard a message six or seven times, something new will suddenly be illuminated within you. All of a sudden it will make sense. The Word of God is new every morning...it's alive and fresh! So, keep planting the Word within you and it will grow and develop.

Every day the devil is coming at you to steal, kill and destroy your self-image. He doesn't come boldly; he comes subtly—with subtle thoughts.

For example, after you witness to someone, the devil will say, "You sounded so stupid." He plants a subtle thought and then you agree with it.

Someone may tell you that you did a great job, but if you continue to think, *I sounded so stupid,* you will believe it and it will be imprinted in your mind.

The bottom line is: your thoughts are what have to change. Take hold of what the Word of God says and believe it more than you believe your own thoughts, more than you believe the thoughts Satan sends your way.

Changing how you think, speak and behave will take time. It won't happen overnight. But if you will apply the truths I'm teaching you, change will come.

But you have to be on your toes. The Word says, *Do not be ignorant of the devil's devices* (II Corinthians 2:11). Don't be blinded to how the devil attacks you.

My old thoughts would tell me, *You are stupid. I can't believe you did that.* But I have been resisting those thoughts by speaking, "Those are not my thoughts." If I meditate on those words that have been spoken to me by the devil, I will take hold of them and they will become the abundance of my heart.

I don't want that. So I must act on the Word every moment of every day—and so should you.

You've got to use the Word when you're driving in your car, when you're at home, when you're right in the midst of a situation with your mate, with someone at work, with a friend, or with your children. That's when you have to do what the Word of God says.

If you're in the midst of a situation and you're having discouraging thoughts that the devil has put in your mind, right away take hold of those thoughts and cut them off at the root. The longer you wait to cut the root, the more the thought will grow and become part of your life, even though it wasn't your thought from the beginning.

### You Can Do This!

You can overcome the poor self-image you have right now. You can change it...exchange it...for God's image. You can see yourself through His eyes.

Remember: There are two basic, simple keys for overcoming a poor self-image.

### Key #1
### WALK BY FAITH

*Call those things that be not as though they are.*
*(Romans 4:17)*

Praise God that He has given you His Word. I call myself a confident woman. Are you confident? *Of course I am. The Word says I am. I'm walking by faith, not by sight. I walk in love, I walk in compassion, and I talk with compassion. I speak what the Word says and what I want in my life.*

When you are growing with God and you suddenly find yourself frustrated and mad at yourself, it's possible that your *Word tank* is low or empty. You went as far as you could on the tank that you had. But now you've got to fill up again. Study the Word and fill up your tank!

You have to believe that the Word is working in you.

You need to have faith in yourself that you are acting

on the Word, even though in some situations you may feel like you aren't moving. Imagine yourself getting filled up regularly. This is why it's so important to be around godly people.

Remember, Key #1: *Walking by faith is using your faith, demanding faith, and living your faith.*

## Key #2
## ACCEPT GOD'S UNCONDITIONAL LOVE

*But God demonstrates His own love toward us, in that while we were still sinners, Christ died for us. (Romans 5:8)*

> Everything can be taken away from a person but the freedom to choose how to react in any given set of circumstances.
> -Victor Frankl

When you were at your worst, Christ died for you. Spend time meditating on this verse. It's natural to try to "work" for God's love or try to "earn" God's love. Too often, we work at trying to make ourselves change and get it together. We try to make ourselves operate in the talents and gifts God has given us. We try to make God live big within us.

We try to change ourselves and overcome on our own. The world tries that all the time, and it does not work. Why should we think now that we're saved we're supposed to do it all by ourselves? We couldn't do it before, so how are we supposed to do it now?

God loves you at your worst. You aren't at your worst

now, but you were just before you were saved. I can remember when I got saved. I remember being a lazy, unmotivated, unhappy person. I didn't have any goals or direction and didn't really care. But God loved me enough to save me anyhow. If God loved us then, why do we try to make Him love us now by doing all the right things?

Now, of course, we're not only trying to make God love us. We're trying to make people love us. We try very hard to make people accept us.

But you and I can't live off of what other people think. It just doesn't work. You have to live off of what God thinks. When I live off what God thinks about me, I don't have to worry whether you love me or not, because I will be walking as God wants me to walk.

## Live In The Acceptance of God

It's so sad that we get into such a vicious cycle and cry out to God, "Will you accept me? Will you accept me? Will you accept me?" You are trying so hard to get Him to accept you, trying to work it out on your own. Then you feel He does not like you as much as you want Him to, so you try even harder.

This is where I believe many Christians struggle. You've met Christians who are totally burned out. They are totally frustrated. And then they blame God for not working in their lives. Do you know why they struggle so? It's because they were doing everything on their own.

They were trying to earn God's acceptance and love and their place in His kingdom when they didn't have to earn it. All they had to do was just live in the acceptance of God.

> *The love of God has been poured out in our hearts by the Holy Spirit who was given to us. For when we were still without strength, in due time Christ died for the ungodly...But God demonstrates His own love toward us, in that while we were still sinners, Christ died for us. (Romans 5:5-8)*

When we were at our worst, Christ died for us. At our best, He died, too. John 15:9 says, **As the Father loved Me, I also have loved you; abide in My love.**

Continue in that love. Don't continue in your works. Don't continue in the thought, *Am I good enough for God?* Don't continue in your own struggles, but *continue in God's love.*

As you do, you will experience a difference in your life. You will go from having a poor self-image to a right self-image. You will go from looking at yourself through a wrong perception to seeing yourself through God's eyes.

# Confess God's Word Over Yourself Today!

*I have the mind of Christ. I choose His higher thoughts and ways. My steps are ordered of the Lord and He makes all things work together for my good as I serve Him. The peace of God guards my heart and mind and He gives me sweet sleep. I do not have a spirit of fear but of power, love and a sound mind. I restrain my tongue and am quick to listen, slow to speak and slow to anger. I open my mouth with wisdom and on my tongue is the law of kindness. I am a virtuous wife and my husband's heart can trust in me. My children will rise up and call me blessed because I have trained them up in the way that they should go. I celebrate the gifts and talents God has placed within each of them. God has put His Spirit in me to bring the Good News to all, freedom to captives, sight to the blind, and healing to the broken hearted. I will boldly step out to accomplish all that God puts before me as I give Him the praise.*

—Koren Leggett

# Questions To Consider

1. Have you experienced "unconditional love" in any of your relationships? Briefly write the names of those people who have loved you unconditionally and explain how you experienced this love from them.

2. List some "thoughts" you have allowed to be planted in your heart that lower your self-image. Find and write out a scripture that shows God's heart toward you in this situation. Confess this scripture every time the negative thought comes to mind.

3. Think about people in your life into whom you can positively "plant" God thoughts. Make a plan to share those "God thoughts" with them this week.

*Wendy with Caleb, Tasha and Micah, and Lydia, Dylan and Mallory Llewellyn.*

*Ok, gang, we're all dressed up...*
*Let's go change our world!*

# Chapter
## NINE

## Your Right Self-Image Isn't Just For You
*God has a greater purpose.*

I'm not on the earth for my own goals, and my own pursuits. I am here for God's plans and His pursuits. I determined many years ago that God is using me to fulfill His purpose and I can do something for Him.

If you will view yourself in this same light, you won't ever look at yourself and think you can't do anything.

That was David's secret—and Gideon's.

David said, "Use me." And he took on the giant.

Gideon shook in his boots, but he turned his situation around. He turned around an entire nation.

God is shaking you, waking you up saying: *"Come on, you mighty person of valor."* He wants you to know that you can make a difference.

Think about Esther.

Esther was scared, but she spoke faith. She said, "I was born for such a time as this." If she had said she couldn't do it, God would have found someone else.

When He comes to you, don't make Him go find someone else.

Accept the challenge. Lay hold your right self-image by faith. Become all that God created you to be...because He has a higher purpose for you.

### You Are An Ambassador For Christ!

God has called you to be an ambassador—someone who is not afraid, unsure or awkward. II Corinthians 5:20 says, ***Now then, we are ambassadors for Christ, as though God were pleading through us: we implore you on Christ's behalf, be reconciled to God.***

*You don't have to be a fantastic hero to do certain things— to compete. You can be just an ordinary chap, sufficiently motivated to reach challenging goals.*
*- Sir Edmund Hillary*

Think of it like being the U.S. Ambassador to a foreign nation. Can you imagine a U.S. ambassador going into a situation unsure or afraid? Of course not. If that were the case, our government would have to replace them or train them to have the knowledge they needed. Our country would have him or her trained so they would be capable of interacting with other dignitaries with power and authority.

Well, you are called an ambassador. Therefore, your job is to make sure you're ready for the job. Be assertive. Get some training, which will increase your ability to walk into your life situations as an ambassador, into every place that you have influence—your family, your job, your neighborhood.

Begin to see yourself as God sees you—a person with authority. You have been called His ambassador on this earth. Begin to walk with confidence, with your head held high.

The first time God talked to me about praying for one of my family members, I was so scared. My brother wasn't born again at the time, and God spoke to my heart and asked if I was ashamed of Him. If not, I was to be bold. I thought, *Okay, I'm God's ambassador.*

How does an ambassador act? With authority. A natural ambassador knows all the power of his country which is backing him as he walks into situations that might make him feel intimidated.

As an ambassador for Christ, I knew that my sufficiency was not of myself. So I walked into this situation with my brother. I can't say that I walked in quite as boldly as I would have liked to, but I did it.

Let us not be satisfied with just giving money. Money is not enough, money can be got, but they need your hearts to love them. So, spread your love everywhere you go; first of all in your own home. Give love to your children, to your wife or husband, to the next door neighbor.
- Mother Teresa

161

After I did what God had instructed me, it gave me strength to do something more. And that's how it works.

There are things you'll be challenged with today as God's ambassador. They will be things you'll do for the first time. You may smile at a person as you walk by them, and say, "God bless you." That's being an ambassador. That's walking in the strength of God's Word. In your workplace, if someone complains about their spouse, you may say, "I'll pray for you." Maybe you'll pray out loud or quietly on your own. Just take a step and rise up in that place of who you are.

## Follow Me As I Follow Christ

When you have a right self-image, people will be drawn to you, and they will want to follow your example.

The Apostle Paul knew this. He said we are to follow him as he followed Christ, (Philippians 3:17).

Personally, I want to be able to say to every single person who knows me, either in words or by my actions, "Follow me as I follow Christ."

If I had an image that said, *I'm no good*, why would anyone want to follow me anywhere? There would be no way I would draw anyone to my Savior. I don't want to come across as a depressed, sad woman. I want to see myself as God sees me and then let the world see God in me.

I want to see myself through God's eyes. I want to be an

excellent ambassador. I want to fulfill God's destiny for me on this earth.

## Your Destiny Is Bigger Than You

Your destiny is bigger than you. Yes, it's to fulfill the specific purposes for your life personally. But the reason you are on this earth is to bring people into the saving knowledge of Jesus Christ. That's being an ambassador—and that's your highest destiny.

*We must not only give what we have, we must also give what we are.*
*- Cardinal Mercia*

If fear or anxiety is rising up within you right now...it's because your self-image has an area that needs to be conformed into God's image.

Telling others about Jesus should never be scary. I John 4:4 says, ***You are of God, little children, and have overcome them, because He who is in you is greater than he who is in the world.*** God, *in you,* is greater! You don't have to be timid, shy, fearful or unsure. You are an ambassador.

Once I was on an airplane coming back from a pastors' conference with Casey, and I sat next to an older woman. I asked her if she was a Christian, and her reply was, "I think so."

I didn't say a word. I didn't respond with, *What do you mean, 'You think so'? You can know if you are born again.*

163

She probably grew up in church. I didn't respond to her need because I did not have the right view of myself. I had my old negative view of inability, *I'm too young. I can't do anything,* instead of God's view.

When we do not see ourselves as God sees us, we do not act as God wants us to act. We miss many opportunities because we don't view ourselves properly.

Whenever there is a need, it doesn't matter what age or sex you are. If there is a need and God has placed you there, when you have the right view of yourself, you will meet that need. If you don't have the right view of yourself, you won't meet that need.

> When you are making a success of something, it is not work. It's a way of life. You enjoy yourself because you are making your contribution to the world.
> - Andy Granatelli

Proverbs 23:7 says, ***For as he thinks in his heart, so is he....***

It isn't who you are, as much as it is who you think you are that determines what you see in yourself.

Sometimes we are timid and wonder if we can do anything because we have not trained ourselves in the Word and in prayer. Why don't you change that negative image of yourself? Learn the Word so you will have the ability to rise up in those situations.

An ambassador who travels around the world trains himself and studies the culture where he will be serving. He must know the language, customs, cultures and situations of the land. He takes the time to learn before he can walk as an ambassador. We should do no less.

Take the time to study the Word. Do something every day to be taught and trained in the Word. Then God can use you in more and more situations. God sets up divine appointments every day. The more you are prepared, the more appointments He can plan for you in your life.

## You Really Are Able

As a believer, you are a mighty ambassador of Christ, and because you are, you have influence. When you acknowledge that you are an ambassador and that you influence people, it makes you straighten up and ask yourself:

❖ What am I saying?

❖ What am I doing?

❖ How am I acting?

❖ What kind of Christian am I?

❖ Am I helping others reach their destiny?

Whether you believe it or not, you've got what it takes! You have God on your side. You have the Word of God to give you a firm foundation and you have yourself! Obviously, since you have read this entire book, you are a person who wants to do something great with your life. You are ready and willing to change, grow and take the next step. God has a wonderful plan for you. I pray and believe you will be all that He has created you to be!

But you have to make the choice to change how you see yourself. It's all in the perspective. It's all in seeing yourself through God's eyes.

Caleb and Joshua had this choice when they went to spy out the Promised Land.

***Then Caleb quieted the people before Moses, and said, "Let us go up at once and take possession, for we are well able to overcome it." But the men who had gone up with him said, "We are not able to go up against the people, for they are stronger than we." And they gave the children of Israel a bad report of the land which they had spied out, saying, "The land through which we have gone as spies is a land that devours its inhabitants, and all the people whom we saw in it are men of great stature. "There we saw the giants (the descendants of Anak came from the giants); and we were like grasshoppers in our own sight, and so we were in their sight".*** *(Numbers 13:30-33)*

Who are you in your own sight? In the sight of the ten spies they were as grasshoppers. So what happened? The only two people from that generation who got to go into the Promised Land were Caleb and Joshua. Why? Because they saw themselves as "well able" and said, "God is with us." They saw themselves through God's eyes.

II Corinthians 3:5 says, ***Not that we are sufficient***

*of ourselves to think of anything as being from ourselves, but our sufficiency is from God.*

Our sufficiency and our ability is from God. We have the ability to do what He has called us to do to complete our destinies in Him. He has equipped us. He has given us the strength, the talents and the means to do it.

## Grasshopper or Ambassador?

In your own sight, are you a grasshopper, or are you an ambassador? In your own sight, are you an ambassador for Christ? Do you understand you have been given the authority, power and the Word of God to be able to go and do?

In their own sight, the spies said there were giants. There *are* giants. Giants of fear, depression, lack, of "I can't do it." There are giants of your past, of things our peers say about us, of our husbands, wives and family members who say, "You can't do it."

Yes, there are giants out there, but you have to ask yourself, "What am I going to do?"

Do you go God's way, or do you live in that place of fear? Do you live in the image of the world? Do you live in the image that the devil has tried to convince you of?

John 10:10 says that if he can deceive you or get you in fear, then he can steal, kill, and destroy the destiny of your life. He can destroy your destiny if you are unwilling to take hold of God's Word.

You can't afford to live with a poor self-image one day longer. You can't afford to live in a position where Satan will be able to kill, steal and destroy in your life.

Make the choice now to be the ambassador God has appointed you to be. Go ahead and take a hold of what God says and begin to learn and grow.

Thirty years ago, I began the process of growing. I had a willing mind and heart. I wanted to renew the spirit of my mind and know who I was in Christ. I didn't want to be a lazy, undisciplined, bossy, or a do-nothing person.

Since then I have been able to take hold of the principles of God's Word and say, *"I see the giant out there, but I know that I am an ambassador, and I've got all of Your authority behind me, Lord. I've got all of Your Words that say I am more than able, that I can do all things through Christ who strengthens me, that greater is He who is in me than he who is in the world. With Your Word, I can drive the giants away."*

Nothing can stand against God's Word. Nothing can beat you when you understand who you are in Christ.

But anything can beat you if you look at your own sufficiency. Anything can make you draw back when you only see it from your own perspective. Although positive confession is good, you can be beaten by positive confession, because it comes from your own sufficiency.

I'm not talking about my own sufficiency or doing things on my own. I have a great image because I want to be a great ambassador on this earth for Christ. I want to see who I am in Christ. I don't have to live in fear of all the things in my future and be dominated by the baggage of my past. I choose to be dominated by God's thoughts, by God's vision and dreams that are within me. I want to go and do, help and serve, and be an influence on this earth. I want to use the gifts and talents that are placed within me in all areas of my life.

*Often we avoid situations and people where the risks of failure and rejection are high. We need to live for Christ rather than for the approval of people.*
*- Dr. Robert S. McGee*

That's what God has for you and me. You can have that. You can walk in that. You can go for that. It does take some work on your part. Not hard work, just diligence and a willing mind that says you are going to learn. I know you can do it. I know what I used to think about myself and now I know what God thinks about me. I no longer see myself as a grasshopper. I no longer see the giants overwhelming me, but I see the overcomer God has created me to be!

II Corinthians 5:20 says, **Now then, we are ambassadors for Christ, as though God were pleading through us: we implore you on Christ's behalf, be reconciled to God.**

Confess the truth about yourself: *I'm not done. My destiny is not complete, and I am going to walk in the fullness of who You've created me to be on this earth. I am going to understand and grow in the gifts and talents that You have placed within me to help and complete others.*

Your gifts and talents were given to you to serve others, not for your own gain. They are to help others improve their spiritual and natural quality of life.

Luke 6:38 says, **Give, and it will be given to you....** What you give out is what will come back to you. If you give away the strength of God's love within you, the strength of His love will come back to you. If you give away security and forgiveness, security and forgiveness will come back to you.

Speak the Word, live the Word, act the Word, and know that you are set on this earth for such a time as this to influence and help people as a mighty ambassador. Don't let things hinder you, but be the mighty person that God has called you to be!

# Confess God's Word Over Yourself Today!

*Thank You, Father, I confidently wear Your favor and peace today like a coat, because by prayer and supplication I make all my requests known to You and Your peace guards my mind and my thoughts. My life winds upward continually as I optimistically look into my future with positive expectancy. I have more than enough time today to do all I choose to do. My priorities are God's priorities and make themselves known to me, as I faithfully choose to act on them. I hear His voice today. I am led by the Spirit, fulfilling His desires. I live today with premeditated purpose. I am in charge and at peace with myself and with others. I choose my attitudes wisely, premeditating the outcomes I desire. I frame my world by the positive God Words of my mouth.*

*—Denise Llewellyn*

# Questions to Consider

Congratulations! I'm not sure you realize how special you are. You are among the few people who have actually completed a book on self-esteem. Most of us think about change, dream about change and say we desire to change. So few ever do anything about it. You are one of those who do!

Take the time to review the previous "Questions To Consider" and write down the areas you have seen growth in your life since you started reading this book—and then write down those areas you would like to continue working on. I believe you will accomplish all that you set your mind to do and that God is working in you to do His good pleasure!

I would love to hear of your victory walk! Drop me a short note and tell me what God has done for you!

## Smile time! Go ahead and laugh out loud!!

*The Rules:*

1. The female always makes the rules.
2. The rules are subject to change at any time without prior notification.
3. No male can possibly know the rules.
4. If the female suspects the male knows all the rules, she must immediately change some of the rules.
5. The female is never wrong.
6. If the female is wrong it is because of a flagrant misunderstanding which was a direct result of something the male did or said wrong.
7. If rule six applies, the male must apologize immediately for causing the misunderstanding.
8. The female can change her mind at any given point.
9. The male must never change his mind without express written consent from the female.
10. The female has every right to be angry or upset at any time.
11. The male must remain calm at all times (unless the female wants him to be angry or upset).
12. The female must under no circumstance let the male know whether or not she wants him to be angry or upset.
13. Any attempt to document these rules could result in bodily harm.
14. If the female has PMS, all rules are null and void.
15. The male cannot diagnose PMS.
16. All males must have a copy of the rules.

*—Author Unknown*

## A Special Message to Men

Men and husbands, when you do not have the image of God being built within you, you will breed insecurity everywhere you go. You will breed it in yourself, in your wife, and in your children. Your self-image produces "destiny" within you. And that sense of destiny then brings satisfaction because you are in the will of God.

When you come home from a day that has been filled with a sense of destiny you are feeling uplifted. That doesn't mean everything is perfect in your job. There have been days when my husband, Casey, has come home weary or fatigued. I don't mean that everything has to be perfect. But, there is a security in knowing you are walking in your destiny. It may still be a challenge at times, but you can overcome the challenges because you are at peace with your destiny.

What if you don't have that sense of destiny in your life? Some of you are walking outside of the gifts, talents and callings that God has put within you. Why? Possibly it is because you are afraid to do what is in your heart to do. You are doing what other people's opinions have told you to do. Is this impossible or can you fix it?

Here are some keys to get back on God's track for your life:

1) Pray and ask God to reveal His calling in your life.
2) Ask the people around you, who know you, what they think.

175

3) Find out what the Word of God says about who you are in Christ.

4) What do you love to do? What is your passion?

## Make The Most of Your Life!

One important thing you can do to fulfill your destiny is read *Fulfilling Your God Given Destiny* by Casey Treat. You need to understand what your destiny is. Don't waste your life. I think a lot of domestic violence comes out of the fact that men are dissatisfied with what they are doing. You are dissatisfied with everything in your life. Nothing is working. It is not working because you are not doing what God has planned for you to do in your life. That doesn't mean to quit your job without getting some direction first. That would be irresponsible. Be responsible, but check it out. Start learning and growing.

## Confess God's Word Over Yourself Today!

*My body is the temple of the Holy Ghost. There shall no evil befall me, neither shall any plague come near my dwelling. By the stripes of Jesus I am healed. I am blessed with the blessings of Abraham. I am very rich in silver and in gold. The blessing of the Lord makes me rich and He adds no sorrow to it. I prosper and live in health even as my soul prospers. As He who has called me is Holy, so I am holy in all manner of lifestyle because it is written, 'Be ye holy as I am holy.' I am renewed in the spirit of my mind and put on the new man which after God is created in righteousness and true holiness. I am strong and very courageous.*

*—Pastor Casey Treat*

# References

Josh McDowell. *His Image, My Image* (Here's Life Publishers, P.O. Box 1576, San Bernardino, CA,. 92402, 1984), p. 42-43.

*The Birth Order Book*, Kevin Leman, (Fleming H. Revell Co., P.O. Box 6287 Grand Rapids, Michigan 49516-6287) Fourth printing, 1999

*Illustrations Unlimited*; Tyndale House Publishers; Wheaton, Illinois. Edited by James S. Hewitt.

*Chicken Soup for the Christian Soul*; Health Communications, Inc.; Deerfield Beach, Florida.

*Women of Character*; Broadman & Holman Publishers, Nashville, Tenn.

*Staying Power*; by Van Crouch; Honor Books, PO Box 55388, Tulsa, Oklahoma, 74155.

*Winning 101*; by Van Crouch; Honor Books, PO Box 55388, Tulsa, Oklahoma  74155.

## How to Be Born Again and Filled With the Holy Spirit

Every person on earth has sinned and is in need of a personal relationship with God. Romans 3:23 says that *all have sinned and fall short of the glory of God.*

To have a personal relationship, you must believe in the Lord Jesus Christ as your Lord and Savior. According to John 3:16, it is through believing in Jesus that you are born again: *For God so loved the world that He gave His only begotten Son, that whoever believes in Him should not perish but have everlasting life.*

When you are born again, you can know God and have everlasting life. John 3:3 says, *Jesus answered and said to him, 'Most assuredly, I say to you, unless one is born again, he cannot see the kingdom of God.'*

Being born again is the gift of God. It cannot be earned, and you cannot achieve it on your own. Romans 6:23 says, *For the wages of sin is death, but the gift of God is eternal life in Christ Jesus our Lord.*

Ephesians 2:8-9 makes it clear: *For it is by grace you have been saved, through faith—and this not from yourselves, it is the gift of God—not by works, so that no one can boast.*

When you are born again, you receive Jesus as your Lord or Master, and you commit yourself to follow His Word (the Bible). Romans 10:9-10 says, *That if you con-*

*fess with your mouth the Lord Jesus and believe in your heart that God has raised Him from the dead, you will be saved. For with the heart one believes unto righteousness, and with the mouth confession is made unto salvation.*

I John 2:3 tells us it is a commitment: *Now by this we know that we know Him, if we keep His commandments.*

If you are ready to make this life-changing commitment, then pray according to Romans 10:9-10:

*God, I come to You in the Name of Jesus. I ask You to come into my life. I confess with my mouth that Jesus is my Lord and I believe in my heart that You have raised Him from the dead. I turn my back on sin and I commit to follow You for the rest of my life. I thank You, Father, for saving me!*

Welcome to the family of Christ! You are now born again, forgiven and on your way to heaven. You are a new creation in Christ Jesus. II Corinthians 5:17 says, *Therefore, if anyone is in Christ, he is a new creation; old things have passed away; behold, all things have become new.*

Yet this is only the beginning of your new life as a Christian. As you study God's Word and apply its truths to your life, you will renew your mind and grow as a Christian.

Romans 12:1-2 says, *I beseech you therefore, breth-*

ren, *by the mercies of God, that you present your bod-ies a living sacrifice, holy, acceptable to God, which is your reasonable service. And do not be conformed to this world, but be transformed by the renewing of your mind, that you may prove what is that good and acceptable and perfect will of God.*

Become a part of a church where the Word of God is preached in truth, and you can be encouraged by other believers. Hebrews 10:25 says, **Not forsaking the as-sembling of ourselves together, as is the manner of some, but exhorting one another, and so much the more as you see the Day approaching.**

If doubts or fears come to your mind that you are not truly born again, reject them and realize that God's Word is what your salvation is based on, not what you think or feel.

Romans 10:9-10, the verses you based your prayer on, say, **That if you confess with your mouth the Lord Jesus and believe in your heart that God has raised Him from the dead, you will be saved. For with the heart one believes unto righteousness, and with the mouth confession is made unto salvation.**

Part of the Christian walk is to publicly acknowledge your decision through being baptized in water. John the Baptist, who was Jesus' cousin, baptized Jesus in the Jordan River. Jesus wants this for you as well. Acts 10:48 says, **And he commanded them to be baptized in the** *name of the Lord.*

To help you succeed on this earth as a Christian, God has also given you the gift of the Holy Spirit. He is your helper.

## Being Filled With the Holy Spirit

The Holy Spirit is your comforter and teacher. He has been given to you to help you in your everyday life. John 14:26 says, *But the Helper, the Holy Spirit, whom the Father will send in My name, He will teach you all things, and bring to your remembrance all things that I said to you.*

The Holy Spirit will give you the power to be a strong witness for Jesus. Acts 1:8 says, *But you shall receive power when the Holy Spirit has come upon you; and you shall be witnesses to Me in Jerusalem, and in all Judea and Samaria, and to the end of the earth.*

When you are filled with the Holy Spirit, you can speak in other tongues for the purpose of prayer, prophesying, worship and personal edification. Acts 2:4 says, *And they were all filled with the Holy Spirit and began to speak with other tongues, as the Spirit gave them utterance.*

The Holy Spirit is for every born again person. You don't have to wait or work to receive Him. Acts 2:38-39 tells us, *Then Peter said to them, 'Repent, and let ev-*

*ery one of you be baptized in the name of Jesus Christ for the remission of sins; and you shall receive the gift of the Holy Spirit. For the promise is to you and to your children, and to all who are afar off, as many as the Lord our God will call.'*

When you receive the Holy Spirit and speak in other tongues, your mind will not understand anything you are saying. It will sound useless and foolish to you, but you are speaking mysteries to God, not to yourself or to other people.

I Corinthians 14:2 says, *For he who speaks in a tongue does not speak to men but to God, for no one understands him; however, in the spirit he speaks mysteries.*

Speaking in tongues is an act of your will. God gives you the ability to do it, but He will not force you or do it for you. I Corinthians 14:14-15 says, *For if I pray in a tongue, my spirit prays, but my understanding is unfruitful. What is the conclusion then? I will pray with the spirit, and I will also pray with the under-standing. I will sing with the spirit, and I will also sing with the understanding.*

If you ask for the Holy Spirit in faith, God the Father will give Him to you: *If you then, being evil, know how to give good gifts to your children, how much more will your heavenly Father give the Holy Spirit to those who ask Him! (Luke 11:13).*

183

Would you like to receive the Holy Spirit today?

If so, pray according to Luke 11:13, asking God to fill you with the Holy Spirit:

*Father, I come to You in the Name of Jesus. I ask You to fill me with Your Holy Spirit. I receive Him from You and according to the Bible I will now pray in other tongues as the Spirit gives me the utterance. Thank You, Father!*

After praying this prayer asking God to fill you, pray confidently in other tongues. As you pray regularly in other tongues, it will build you up and charge up your spirit man. Jude 1:20 says, *But you, beloved, building yourselves up on your most holy faith, praying in the Holy Spirit.*

As you live your Christian walk, read God's Word and renew your mind according to what it says. Then you will be able to live a powerful life as a believer. Romans 12:1-2 instructs us saying, *I beseech you therefore, brethren, by the mercies of God, that you present your bodies a living sacrifice, holy, acceptable to God, which is your reasonable service. And do not be conformed to this world, but be transformed by the renewing of your mind, that you may prove what is that good and acceptable and perfect will of God.*

184

## How to Recommit Your Life to Christ

If you have made Jesus the Lord of your life, but have fallen away from living a Christian life, you can recommit your life to God. Simply confess and admit your sin to Him. He is faithful to forgive.

I John 1:9 says, *If we confess our sins, He is faithful and just to forgive us our sins and to cleanse us from all unrighteousness.*

Once you confess your sins and receive God's forgiveness, thank Him for forgiving you. He is a just and loving God.

Next, seek out a Bible-believing and teaching church. You need to be trained in the Word of God so you can grow in your Christian walk. Romans 12:1-2 says, *I beseech you therefore, brethren, by the mercies of God, that you present your bodies a living sacrifice, holy, acceptable to God, which is your reasonable service. And do not be conformed to this world, but be transformed by the renewing of your mind, that you may prove what is that good and acceptable and perfect will of God.*

When Jesus left this earth, He sent the Holy Spirit to help you succeed as a believer in this earth. Have you received Him?

If you have prayed to be born again, to recommit your life, or to be filled with the Holy Spirit, please write to us and tell us. We would love to hear from you. You may write to us at: Christian Faith Center, PO Box 98800, Seattle, Washington 98198, or check out our Web site at www.caseytreat.com or www.wendytreat.com.

—Casey and Wendy Treat

# About the Author

Wendy Treat is a real wife with real children and real friends, who lives the principles taught in the Word in a real world. She is a real person who received Christ into her life and was filled with the Holy Spirit in 1974. Wendy met her husband, Casey, in 1976, while attending Bible School.

She and Casey married in 1978, and have three children. They founded Christian Faith Center in Seattle, Washington, in 1980 and continue to pastor their thriving congregation of one church with two locations. Their television program, *Living On Course*, is seen in the United States and abroad.

A respected speaker and author, Wendy believes that a right self-image is key to a successful life—and to fulfilling your destiny. Therefore, she loves to encourage everyone she touches as she lives, preaches and teaches how to see yourself through God's eyes.

For information on Teaching Materials
by Casey and Wendy Treat  contact us at:
P.O. Box 98800 Seattle, Washington 98198
Or call 1-888-2WISDOM
Order online at: www.caseytreat.com
and www.wendytreat.com

7290629R0

Made in the USA
Lexington, KY
14 November 2010